HEALING THE CHILD WITHIN

Discovery and Recovery
for Adult Children
of Dysfunctional Families

Charles L. Whitfield, M.D.

Health Communications, Inc.
Deerfield Beach, Florida

Charles L. Whitfield, M.D.
Box 420487
Atlanta, GA 30342
404-843-4300

Library of Congress Cataloging-in-Publication Data

Whitfield, Charles L.
  Healing the child within.

  Bibliography: p.
  1. Co-dependence (Psychology) — Treatment. 2. Self.
3. Alcoholics — Family relationships. 4. Children of
alcoholic parents — Mental health. 5. Adult child abuse victims
— Mental health. I. Title.
  RC569.5.C63W47   1987   616.89   87-137

Reprinted 1989

© 1987   Charles L. Whitfield

ISBN 0-932194-40-0

Published by Health Communications, Inc.
            Enterprise Center
            3201 Southwest 15th Street
            Deerfield Beach, FL 33442

Cover Design and Illustration by Reta Thomas

ABOUT THE AUTHOR

Charles Whitfield is a physician who specializes in helping people who are alcoholic, chemical dependent or co-dependent, and adult children of troubled or dysfunctional families. He has also worked, and continues to work on healing his own child within.

Dr. Charles Whitfield is in private practice in Atlanta and is a founding board member of the National Association for Children of Alcoholics. He is on the faculty of Rutgers Summer School of Advanced Alcohol Studies. He is the author of the other books shown below, and lectures and does workshops nationally. To be on his mailing list for these workshops in your area, please send a self-addressed stamped envelope to: Box 420487, Atlanta, GA 30342, (404) 843-4300.

Charles Whitfield's other books include:

A Gift to Myself: a personal workbook and guide to healing the child within

Co-dependence: Healing the Human Condition

Boundaries and Relationships: Knowing, Protecting and Enjoying the Self

Memory and Abuse: Remembering and Healing the Wounds of Trauma

Alcoholism and Spirituality (preprint form only)

My Recovery Plan (three booklets on each of the stages of recovery)

ACKNOWLEDGMENTS

Special thanks to the following who read an early draft of this book and offered constructive suggestions: Herb Gravitz, Julie Bowden, Vicki Mermelstein, Rebecca Peres, Jerry Hunt, John Femino, Jeanne Harper, Barbara Ensor, Lucy Robe, John Davis, Doug Hedrick, Mary Jackson, Barry Tuchfeld, Bob Subby, and Anne Wilson Schaef.

Grateful acknowledgment is given to the following for permission to reprint: Portia Nelson's "Autobiography in Five Short Chapters." Copyright Portia Nelson, 1980, reprinted The Popular Library Edition "There's a Hole in my Sidewalk," copyright 1977, permission in process. Arthur Deikman's quote from his book **The Observing Self,** copyright 1972 by Beacon Press, Boston. Alice Miller's quote from her book **Thou Shalt Not Be Aware,** copyright 1984 by Alice Miller, published by Farrar Straus Giroux, New York. Bruce Fischer's illustration "Cycle of Shame and Compulsive Behavior," copyright Bruce Fischer, 1986. American Psychiatric Association's **"Severity Rating of Psychosocial Stressors,"** from DSM-III, copyright 1980 American Psychiatric Association. In modified form, Al-Anon Family Groups Questions for Adult Children of Alcoholics, Madison Sq. Station, New York, 1985. The poem "Please Hear What I'm Not Saying," copyright 1966 by Charles C. Finn. Anonymous author's poem "Afraid of Night," by permission of the author. Timmen Cermak's quotes from his book **Diagnosing and Treating Co-dependence,** copyright 1986 by the Johnson Institute.

DEDICATION

This book is dedicated to the Child Within each of us.

CONTENTS

1. Introduction 1

2. Background of the Concept of
   the Child Within 5

3. What is the Child Within? 9

4. Stifling the Child Within 17

5. Parental Conditions that Tend to
   Stifle the Child Within 25

6. The Dynamics of Shame and
   Low Self-Esteem 43

7. The Role of Stress:
   The Post Traumatic Stress Disorder 55

8. How Can We Heal Our Child Within? 59

9. Beginning to Deal With Core Issues 67

10. Identifying and Experiencing
    Our Feelings 77

11. The Process of Grieving 85

12. Continuing to Grieve:
    Risking, Sharing and Telling Our Story 95

13. Transforming 107

14. Integrating 119

15. The Role of Spirituality 127

Appendix 142

References 144

TABLES AND FIGURES

TABLES

1. Some Characteristics of the Real Self and the Co-dependent Self 10
2. A Hierarchy of Human Needs 18
3. Parental Conditions Associated with Dynamics of Adult Children of Alcoholics and Other Dysfunctional Families 26
4. Some Definitions of Co-dependence 29
5. Some Terms for Mental, Emotional, and Spiritual Trauma That May Be Experienced by Children and Adults 40
6. Negative Rules and Negative Messages Commonly Heard in Alcoholic or Other Troubled Families 47
7. Severity Rating of Psychosocial Stressors 56
8. Levels of Awareness and Communication of Feelings, With Guidelines for Sharing 81
9. Some Feelings and Their Opposites 84
10. Some Examples of Loss 88
11. Some Losses in Alcoholism, etc. 90
12. Answers, Approaches and Strategies often Used to Protect the Parents 102
13. Some Steps in Transforming and Integrating Recovery Issues in Healing our Child Within 109
14. Similar Hierarchies of Human Needs, Development and Consciousness 129
15. Levels of Being, Awareness or Consciousness of Our Child Within 130
16. Defining Some Clinical Therapeutic Properties of the Self 135

FIGURES

1. Cycle of Shame and Compulsive Behavior 50
2. Our Story 98
3. Healing Process for the Child Within 120
4. Co-Creating Our Story 122
5. Recovery & Growth Through Experiencing, Telling Our Story and Observing It 124
6. Relationship of the Observing Self and the Self 136

Chapter 1

Discovering
Our Child Within

Introduction

The concept of the Child Within has been a part of our world culture for at least two thousand years. Carl Jung called it the "Divine Child" and Emmet Fox called it the "Wonder Child." Psychotherapists Alice Miller and Donald Winnicott refer to it as the "true self." Rokelle Lerner and others in the field of chemical dependence call it the "inner child."

The Child Within refers to that part of each of us which is ultimately alive, energetic, creative and fulfilled; it is our Real Self — who we truly are.

With our parents' unknowing help and society's assistance, most of us deny our Inner Child. When this Child Within is not nurtured or allowed freedom of expression, a false or co-dependent self emerges. We begin to live our lives from a victim stance, and experience difficulties in resolving emotional traumas. The gradual accumulation of unfinished mental and emotional business can lead to chronic anxiety, fear, confusion, emptiness and unhappiness.

Denial of the Child Within and the subsequent emergence of a co-dependent self are particularly common among children and adults who grew up in troubled families, such as those where chronic physical or mental illness, rigidity, coldness or lack of nurturing were common.

Yet, there is a way out. There is a way to discover and to heal our Child Within and to break free of the bondage and suffering of our co-dependent or false self. That is what this book is about.

Will This Book Help Me?

Not everyone was mistreated or abused as a child. No one really knows how many people grow up with a healthy amount and quality of love, guidance and other nurturing. I estimate perhaps 5 to 20%. This means that from 80 to 95% of people did not receive the love, guidance and other nurturing necessary to form consistently healthy relationships, and to feel good about themselves and about what they do.

While not easy to determine whether you lean toward being more healthy or less healthy in relationships with self and others, you may find it helpful to answer some of the following questions.

I call it the "Recovery Potential Survey" because it reflects not only our woundedness, but also the potential that we have to grow and to realize an alive, adventurous and happy life.

Recovery Potential Survey

Circle or check the word that most applies to how you *truly* feel.

1) Do you seek approval and affirmation?
   Never   Seldom   Occasionally   Often   Usually
2) Do you fail to recognize your accomplishments?
   Never   Seldom   Occasionally   Often   Usually
3) Do you fear criticism?
   Never   Seldom   Occasionally   Often   Usually
4) Do you overextend yourself?
   Never   Seldom   Occasionally   Often   Usually
5) Have you had problems with your own compulsive behavior?
   Never   Seldom   Occasionally   Often   Usually
6) Do you have a need for perfection?
   Never   Seldom   Occasionally   Often   Usually
7) Are you uneasy when your life is going smoothly?
   Do you continually anticipate problems?
   Never   Seldom   Occasionally   Often   Usually
8) Do you feel more alive in the midst of a crisis?
   Never   Seldom   Occasionally   Often   Usually

9) Do you care for others easily, yet find it difficult to care for yourself?

Never   Seldom   Occasionally   Often   Usually

10) Do you isolate yourself from other people?

Never   Seldom   Occasionally   Often   Usually

11) Do you respond with anxiety to authority figures and angry people?

Never   Seldom   Occasionally   Often   Usually

12) Do you feel that individuals and society in general are taking advantage of you?

Never   Seldom   Occasionally   Often   Usually

13) Do you have trouble with intimate relationships?

Never   Seldom   Occasionally   Often   Usually

14) Do you attract and seek people who tend to be compulsive?

Never   Seldom   Occasionally   Often   Usually

15) Do you cling to relationships because you are afraid of being alone?

Never   Seldom   Occasionally   Often   Usually

16) Do you often mistrust your own feelings and the feelings expressed by others?

Never   Seldom   Occasionally   Often   Usually

17) Do you find it difficult to express your emotions?

Never   Seldom   Occasionally   Often   Usually

If you answered "occasionally," "often," or "usually" to any of these questions, you may find it useful to continue reading. (These questions are modified from Al-Anon Family Group, 1984, with permission.)

Other questions to consider are:

18) Do you fear any of the following:
   - losing control?

Never   Seldom   Occasionally   Often   Usually

   - your own feelings?

Never   Seldom   Occasionally   Often   Usually

   - conflict and criticism?

Never   Seldom   Occasionally   Often   Usually

   - being rejected or abandoned?

Never   Seldom   Occasionally   Often   Usually

   - being a failure?

Never   Seldom   Occasionally   Often   Usually

19) Is it difficult for you to relax and have fun?

Never   Seldom   Occasionally   Often   Usually

20) Do you find yourself compulsively eating, working, drinking, using drugs, or seeking excitement?

Never   Seldom   Occasionally   Often   Usually

21) Have you tried counseling or psychotherapy, yet still feel that "something" is wrong or missing?

Never   Seldom   Occasionally   Often   Usually

22) Do you frequently feel numb, empty, or sad?
    Never   Seldom   Occasionally   Often   Usually

23) Is it hard for you to trust others?
    Never   Seldom   Occasionally   Often   Usually

24) Do you have an over-developed sense of responsibility?
    Never   Seldom   Occasionally   Often   Usually

25) Do you feel a lack of fulfillment in life, both personally and in your work?
    Never   Seldom   Occasionally   Often   Usually

26) Do you have feelings of guilt, inadequacy or low self-esteem?
    Never   Seldom   Occasionally   Often   Usually

27) Do you have a tendency toward having chronic fatigue, aches and pains?
    Never   Seldom   Occasionally   Often   Usually

28) Do you find that it is difficult to visit your parents for more than a few minutes or a few hours?
    Never   Seldom   Occasionally   Often   Usually

29) Are you uncertain about how to respond when people ask about your feelings?
    Never   Seldom   Occasionally   Often   Usually

30) Have you ever wondered if you might have been mistreated, abused, or neglected as a child?
    Never   Seldom   Occasionally   Often   Usually

31) Do you have difficulty asking for what you want from others?
    Never   Seldom   Occasionally   Often   Usually

If you answered "Occasionally," "Often," or "Usually" to any of these questions, this book may be helpful to you. (If you answered mostly "Never," you may not be aware of some of your feelings.)

In this book, I describe some basic principles of discovering who we really are, and propose that the answer lies in the liberation of our Real or True Self, our Child Within. I will then describe how to bring about the recovery of our Real Self, which may diminish our confusion, pain and suffering.

Accomplishing these tasks will take time, effort and discipline. Because of this, you may wish to read these chapters over at intervals through the coming months and years.

Chapter 2

Background of the Concept of the Child Within

References to the concept of the Child Within originate as far back as before the time of Christ. But three recent developments are important to its current concept.

Child Abuse and Neglect

The first development comes out of two movements. One is the child abuse movement. The other is an offshoot of an interaction of this with certain clinicians and writers in the psychotherapy field. These concepts have evolved over the past 50 years, perhaps coincidentally within the same time frame of the second major movement of the Child Within.

That second major development includes the 12-Step self-help recovery movement and the closely aligned alcohol-and-the-family treatment movement. This may surprise people who are not familiar with all three of these areas: child abuse, psychotherapy and alcoholism recovery. Yet there is a definite interconnection, with each making important contributions.

Alcoholism Recovery

Successful alcoholism recovery began in 1935 with the founding of the fellowship of Alcoholics Anonymous. In addition to suffering from the illness of alcoholism, most founders of AA were either adult children of alcoholics, or were mistreated or abused as children. Many had unsuccessfully tried various forms of psychotherapy. Unfortunately, even today, outside of the field of alcoholism treatment, individual psychotherapy for alcoholics and their family members early in recovery has not substantially improved.

Like psychotherapy, the field of child abuse and neglect is only beginning to discover the vast clinical skills and effectiveness available in the field of alcoholism, other chemical dependence, and co-dependence (defined on page 29). In turn, the alcoholism field is learning more and more from psychotherapy with child abuse and neglect.

During its first 20 years, Alcoholics Anonymous grew rapidly, and became firmly established as *the* "treatment" for alcoholism (Kurtz, 1979). Its 12-Steps of recovery were a revelation for the heretofore misunderstood and mistreated alcoholic. In the mid 1950s both the generic family therapy movement and the fellowship of Al-Anon — which is for the family and friends of alcoholics — came into being. But the *children* in the alcoholic family were given little attention, especially the Child Within of all affected.

Until the late 1960s essentially no articles or books seriously addressed concern for children from alcoholic families. The first book, *The Forgotten Children*, by Margaret Cork, was published in 1969. With that the literature and attention gradually increased.

The Family and Children

During the late 1970s and early '80s, practical approaches to understanding and helping family members of alcoholics and other chemical dependent people soon emerged. The field has developed so rapidly that today some clinicians and educators are specializing in this area. The founding in 1983 of the National Association for Children of Alcoholics (NACoA) encouraged networking and the dissemination of information. At the same time, the first self-help groups for adult children of alcoholics began to meet. Today, these "ACA" or "ACoA" groups are growing so fast that an estimated one new group is started in the USA every day (Cermak, 1985; ACA, 1985; Al-Anon, 1986).

During these last few decades and years, the concept of the

Child Within re-emerged and began to mature, both in the alcoholism-family field and in that of psychotherapy.

Psychotherapy

The involvement of psychotherapy in the "Child Within" concept began with the discovery of the human unconscious, followed by Freud's trauma theory. However, Freud quickly discarded the latter for one less clinically effective in healing childhood trauma wounds — the drive (or instinct) theory and the Oedipus complex (Freud, 1964; Miller, 1983; 1984). While many of Freud's brightest and most creative students and colleagues, such as Jung, Adler, Rank, and Assagioli, disagreed with Freud's latter two theories and made their own valuable contributions to the field of psychotherapy, the concept of the "Child Within" — the Real or True Self — came slowly. Contributions by Erikson, Klein, Horney, Sullivan, Fairbairn, Hartman, Jacobson and others paved the way for London pediatrician Donald Winnicott to describe his observations of mothers, infants and children. These included specifics about the Real or True Self, which is our Child Within, and which is crucial in our lives and to *feeling* alive.

Drawing from the psychoanalytic psychotherapy literature, especially from Freud and Winnicott, from observations of her patients, and from reading works on child abuse, in 1979 Alice Miller began integrating child mistreatment, abuse and neglect, and psychoanalytic psychotherapy. In her three books, however, only twice does she make the important connection of alcoholism as a major parental condition predisposing damage to the Child Within, this despite the fact that many of her patients — and those of her psychoanalytic colleagues — were probably children of alcoholics and of co-dependents. In no way do I fault her, for I believe that she has had the same incomplete education that I and most helping professionals had — *i.e.*, essentially no training in alcoholism and co-dependence as primary illnesses (Whitfield, 1980). In fact, our training has actually been *negative* about these two common clinical conditions.

Medical Illness

Another contribution to healing the Child Within came from

using group psychotherapy and guided imagery as a treatment aid for cancer patients. Discovery that many cancer patients had neglected getting their needs met and expressing their feelings, Mathews-Simonton and others (1983) described approaches to remedying these needs. Others in the field of medicine are beginning to use similar approaches in treating heart disease and other life-threatening conditions (Dossey, 1984; Moss, 1985; Siegel, 1986). I believe that the principles and techniques in healing our Child Within can have important and useful applications in helping to ameliorate all illness and suffering.

Spirituality

The final area that connects those above with the Child Within is that of spirituality. The alcoholism and alcoholism-family fields use this recovery aid effectively. Some psychotherapists and physicians are beginning to recognize its value (Wilber, 1979, 1983; Whitfield, 1985; Wegscheider-Cruse, 1985; Kunz, 1985; Moss, 1985; Siegel, 1986; Vaughan, 1985; Bowden, Gravitz, 1987). I refer to spirituality — not organized religion — throughout this book, especially in Chapter 15. As I wrote in *Alcoholism and Spirituality*, I believe that spirituality is crucial in achieving full recovery from any medical or psychological condition, and especially for discovering and ultimately liberating the "Child Within," our Real and True Self.

Just what is our "Child Within?" How do we know it when we see it, feel it or recognize it? What relevance does it have to recovery from the above-mentioned conditions, as well as from other physical, mental-emotional and spiritual illnesses?

Chapter 3

What Is The Child Within?

No matter how distant, evasive, or even alien it may seem to be, we each have a "Child Within" — the part of us that is ultimately alive, energetic, creative and fulfilled. This is our Real Self — who we truly are. Horney, Masterson and others call it the "real self." Some psychotherapists, including Winnicott and Miller, call it the "true self." Some clinicians and educators, in and out of the alcoholism and family fields, also call it the "inner child."

With the help of parents, other authority figures, and institutions (such as education, organized religion, politics, the media, and even psychotherapy), most of us learn to stifle or deny our Child Within. When this vital part of each of us is not nurtured and allowed freedom of expression, a false or co-dependent self emerges. I further describe these two parts of each of us in Table 1. (See page 10).

Our Child Within or Real Self

In this book I use the following terms interchangeably: Real Self, True Self, Child Within, Inner Child, Divine Child, and Higher Self. (I capitalize the first letters to show its importance for us in living and to help differentiate it from the false or lower self.) It has also been called our Deepest Self, our Inner Core (James, Savary, 1977). These items refer to the same core part in us. One description: who we are when we feel most authentic, genuine or spirited.

TABLE 1. Some Characteristics of the Real Self and the Co-dependent Self.

Real Self	Co-Dependent Self
Authentic Self	Unauthentic Self, mask
True Self	False Self, persona
Genuine	Ungenuine, "as-if" personality
Spontaneous	Plans and plods
Expansive, loving	Contracting, fearful
Giving, communicating	Withholding
Accepting of self and others	Envious, critical, idealized, perfectionistic
Compassionate	Other-oriented, overly conforming
Loves Unconditionally	Loves conditionally
Feels feelings, including appropriate, spontaneous, current anger	Denies or hides feelings, including long-held anger (resentment)
Assertive	Aggressive and/or passive
Intuitive	Rational, logical
Child Within, Inner Child Ability to be child like	Over-developed parent/adult scripts; may be childish
Needs to play and have fun	Avoids play and fun
Vulnerable	Pretends always to be strong
Powerful in true sense	Limited power
Trusting	Distrusting
Enjoys being nurtured	Avoids being nurtured
Surrenders	Controls, withdraws
Self-indulgent	Self-righteous
Open to the unconscious	Blocks unconscious material
Remembers our Oneness	Forgets our Oneness; feels separate
Free to grow	Tends to act out unconscious often painful patterns repeatedly
Private self	Public self

Our Real Self is spontaneous, expansive, loving, giving, and communicating. Our True Self accepts ourselves and others. It feels, whether the feelings may be joyful or painful. And it expresses those feelings. Our Real Self accepts our feelings without judgment and fear, and allows them to exist as a valid way of assessing and appreciating life's events.

Our Child Within is expressive, assertive, and creative. It can be childlike in the highest, most mature, and evolved sense of the word. It needs to play and to have fun. And yet it is vulnerable, perhaps because it is so open and trusting. It surrenders to itself, to others and ultimately to the universe. And yet it is powerful in the true sense of power (discussed in Chapters 11 & 15). It is healthily self-indulgent, taking pleasure in receiving and in being nurtured. It is also open to that vast and mysterious part of us that we call our unconscious. It pays attention to the messages that we receive daily from the unconscious, such as dreams, struggles and illness.

By being real, it is free to grow. And while our co-dependent self forgets, our Real Self remembers our Oneness with others and with the universe. Yet for most of us, our Real Self is also our private self. Who knows why we chose not to share? Perhaps it is a fear of being hurt or being rejected. Some have estimated that we show our True Self to others on average for only about 15 minutes each day. For whatever reasons, we tend to keep that part of us private.

When we "come from" or when we *are* our True Self, we feel alive. We may feel pain in the form of hurt, sadness, guilt or anger, but we nonetheless feel *alive*. Or we may feel joy, in the form of contentment, happiness, inspiration or even ecstasy. Overall, we tend to feel current, complete, finished, appropriate, real, whole and sane. We feel alive.

Our Child Within flows naturally from the time we are born to the time that we die and during all of our times and transitions in between. We don't have to *do* anything to be our True Self. It just *is*. If we simply let it be, it will express itself with no particular effort on our part. Indeed, any effort is usually in denying our awareness and expression of it.

Our False or Co-dependent Self

By contrast, another part of us generally feels uncomfortable, strained, or unauthentic. I use the following terms interchangeably: false self, co-dependent self, unauthentic or public self.

Our false self is a cover-up. It is inhibited, contracting and fearful. It is our egocentric ego and super-ego, forever planning and plodding, continually selfish and withholding. It is envious, critical, idealized, blaming, shaming and perfectionistic.

Alienated from the True Self, our false self is other-oriented, i.e., focuses on what it *thinks* others want it to be; it is over-conforming. It gives its love only conditionally. It covers up, hides or denies feelings. Even so, it may make up false feelings, as it often does when we consistently answer a "How are you?" with a perfunctory "I'm just fine." This quick response is often necessary or helpful to defend against the frightening awareness of the false self, which either doesn't know how it feels or does know and has censured these feelings as "wrong" or "bad."

Rather than be appropriately assertive — for the Real Self — it is often either inappropriately aggressive and/or passive.

Our false self tends to be the "critical parent," should we use transactional analysis script terminology. It avoids playing and having fun. It pretends to be "strong" or even "powerful." Yet its power is only minimal or non-existent, and it is in reality unusually fearful, distrusting and destructive.

Because our co-dependent self needs to withdraw and to be in control, it sacrifices nurturing or being nurtured. It cannot surrender. It is self-righteous and attempts to block information coming from the unconscious. Even so, it tends to repeatedly act out unconscious, often painful patterns. Because it forgets our Oneness, it feels separate. It is our public self who we think others and eventually even *we* think we should be.

Most of the time, in the role of our false or co-dependent self, we feel uncomfortable, numb, empty or in a contrived state. *We do not feel real, complete, whole or sane.* At one level or another, we sense that something is wrong, something is missing.

Paradoxically, we often feel like this false self is our natural state, the way we "should be." This could be our addiction or attachment to being that way. We become so accustomed to being our co-dependent self that our Real Self feels guilty, like something is wrong, that we shouldn't feel real and alive. To consider changing this problem is frightening.

This false or co-dependent self appears to be universal among humans. It has been described or referred to countless times in print and in our daily lives. It has been called such diverse names as a survival tool, psychopathology, the egocentric ego and the impaired or defensive self (Masterson, 1985). It can be destructive to self, others and intimate relationships. However, it is a double-edged sword. It has some uses. But just how useful is it? And under what circumstances?

The following poem by Charles C. Finn describes many of our struggles with our false self.

Please Hear What I'm Not Saying

Don't be fooled by me.
Don't be fooled by the face I wear.
For I wear a mask, a thousand masks,
masks that I'm afraid to take off,
and none of them is me.
Pretending is an art that's second nature with me,
but don't be fooled.
For God's sake don't be fooled.
I give you the impression that I'm secure,
that all is sunny and unruffled with me, within as well
    as without,
that confidence is my name and coolness my game,
that the water's calm and I'm in command,
and that I need no one.
But don't believe me.
My surface may seem smooth but my surface is my mask,
ever-varying and ever-concealing.
Beneath lies no complacence.
Beneath lies confusion and fear and aloneness.
But I hide this. I don't want anybody to know it.

I panic at the thought of my weakness and fear
    being exposed.
That's why I frantically create a mask to hide behind,
a nonchalant sophisticated facade,
to help me pretend,
to shield me from the glance that knows.
But such a glance is precisely my salvation.
    My only hope and I know it.
That is, if it's followed by acceptance,
if it's followed by love.
It's the only thing that can liberate me from myself,
from my own self-built prison walls,
from the barriers I so painstakingly erect.
It's the only thing that will assure me of what I can't
    assure myself,
that I'm really worth something.

But I don't tell you this. I don't dare. I'm afraid to.
I'm afraid your glance will not be followed by acceptance,
will not be followed by love.
I'm afraid you'll think less of me, that you'll laugh,
and your laugh would kill me.
I'm afraid that deep-down I'm nothing, that I'm just
    no good,
and that you will see this and reject me.

So I play my game, my desperate pretending game,
with a facade of assurance without
and a trembling child within.
So begins the glittering but empty parade of masks,
and my life becomes a front.
I idly chatter to you in the suave tones of surface talk.
I tell you everything that's really nothing,
and nothing of what's everything,
of what's crying within me.
So when I'm going through my routine,
do not be fooled by what I'm saying.
Please listen carefully and try to hear what I'm not saying,
what I'd like to be able to say,
what for survival I need to say,
but what I can't say.

I don't like to hide.
I don't like to play superficial phony games.
I want to stop playing them.
I want to be genuine and spontaneous and me,
but you've got to help me.
You've got to hold out your hand
even when that's the last thing I seem to want.
Only you can wipe away from my eyes the blank stare of the
    breathing dead.
Only you can call me into aliveness.
Each time you're kind and gentle and encouraging,
each time you try to understand because you really care,
my heart begins to grow wings,
very small wings,

very feeble wings,
but wings!
With your power to touch me into feeling
you can breathe life into me.
I want you to know that.

I want you to know how important you are to me,
how you can be a creator — a honest-to-God creator —
of the person that is me
if you choose to.
You alone can break down the wall behind which I tremble,
you alone can remove my mask,
you alone can release me from my shadow-world of panic
    and uncertainty, from my lonely prison,
if you choose to.
Please choose to. Do not pass me by.
It will not be easy for you.

A long conviction of worthlessness builds strong walls.
The nearer you approach to me
the blinder I may strike back.
It's irrational, but despite what the books say about man,
often I am irrational.
I fight against the very thing that I cry out for.
But I am told that love is stronger than strong walls,
and in this lies my hope.
Please try to beat down those walls
with firm hands
but with gentle hands
for a child is very sensitive.

Who am I, you may wonder?
I am someone you know very well.
For I am every man you meet
and I am every woman you meet.

Chapter 4

Stifling the Child Within

How do our parents, other authority figures and institutions — such as education, organized religion, politics, the media, and even the helping professions — stifle or deny our Child Within? How can we identify whether *we* were affected? What factors or conditions made our parents and others stifle our Child?

Some Human Needs

In ideal circumstances, some human needs must be fulfilled so that our Child Within can develop and grow. Drawing on authors such as Maslow (1962), Weil (1973), Miller (1983, 1984), and Glasser (1985), I compiled a hierarchical list of twenty factors or conditions that I call "human needs" (See Table 2). Nearly all are associated with our relationship with ourself and with people around us.

To reach our full potential, we apparently require most of these needs. Growing up in an environment without these needs, we grow up automatically without realizing that our needs have not been met and are not being met. We often feel confused and chronically unhappy.

Survival, Safety and Security

A newborn requires so much attention that someone must be

TABLE 2. A Hierarchy of Human Needs (Compiled in part from Maslow, 1962; Miller, 1981; Weil, 1973; Glasser, 1985).

---

1. Survival
2. Safety
3. Touching, skin contact
4. Attention
5. Mirroring and echoing
6. Guidance
7. Listening
8. Being real
9. Participating
10. Acceptance
    Others are aware of, take seriously and admire the Real You
    Freedom to be the Real You
    Tolerance of your feelings
    Validation
    Respect
    Belonging and love
11. Opportunity to grieve losses and to grow
12. Support
13. Loyalty and trust
14. Accomplishment
    Mastery, "Power," "Control"
    Creativity
    Having a sense of completion
    Making a contribution
15. Altering one's state of consciousness, transcending the ordinary
16. Sexuality
17. Enjoyment or fun
18. Freedom
19. Nurturing
20. Unconditional love (including connection with a Higher Power)

---

available and able to provide enough needs for its simple survival. At the barest minimum, this includes its safety and security.

Touching

From studies by Spitz, Montague and others we know the importance of touching is a human need. Infants deprived of touching fail to thrive and grow, even if they get proper food, nourishment and protection. Touching is most powerful by appropriate skin to skin contact. Experiments with rabbits fed atherosclerosis-inducing diets show that those rabbits which are held and petted by the laboratory workers tend not to get atherosclerosis (hardening of the arteries). Those rabbits which are *not* held and petted tend to get atherosclerosis (Dossey, 1985).

It seems that to feel connected and cared for, we need to be hugged and touched. Virginia Satir has suggested that we need from four to twelve hugs a day as part of our health maintenance.

Attention

The child or individual must be attended to, *i.e.*, given attention. The mother or other parent figure(s) must attend the infant and child so that at least its safety, security and touching are met.

Mirroring and Echoing

The next need begins to validate the infant, child or even the adult, as a feeling and thinking being. Mirroring and echoing is when the mother reacts non-verbally by facial expression, posture, sounds and other movements so that it realizes that it is understood.

At this point we understand that if the mother or other parent figure cannot provide these first few needs, the child's physical, mental-emotional and spiritual growth would likely be stunted. One reason may be that the mother herself is so impoverished and needy that she *uses* her infant to satisfy her own unmet needs. This is an amazing thing about infants. They can sense that mother is needy, and can eventually detect her *specific* needs and *begin providing them for her.* Of course, this carries a major price — the denial, stifling and stunting of the infant's own True Self or Child Within. That price escalates as the child grows into an adult, with resulting physical, mental-emotional and spiritual suffering.

Guidance

Guidance, also a part of helping the infant and child to develop and grow, may include advice, assistance, and any other form of help, verbal or non-verbal. It also includes modeling and teaching appropriate and healthy social skills.

Listening, Participating and Accepting

It is helpful to know that someone hears us, even if they do not always understand. Increasingly nourishing forms or types of listening are associated with numbers 9 through 20 on this Needs Hierarchy, including participation with the child in appropriate activities, and *accepting* the Self — the Child Within — of the infant, child and eventual adult. The mother, other parent figure or concerned other is aware of, takes seriously and admires the other person's Real Self. They demonstrate their acceptance by respecting, validating, and being tolerant of the *feelings* of the other's Real Self. This allows the Child Within the freedom to be its authentic Self and to grow.

Now, readers may see that some of their needs were not — perhaps are not — being met. Yet we are but half-way through this hierarchy of our human needs.

Opportunity To Grieve Losses and To Grow

With each loss that we experience, whether it be a real or a threatened loss, we have a need to grieve it, *i.e.*, to work through the associated pain and suffering. To do so takes time. And when we grieve our losses to completion, we grow. This process of grieving and growing is what a major part of this book is about.

Support

Support implies that the friend or caretaker will not block the Real Self's seeking, receiving input and creating, and will do everything possible to assure that the Real Self can fulfill its potential. Support includes actively doing whatever is possible to see that the Real Self is able to fulfill its potential.

Loyalty and Trust

Being supportive requires loyalty and trust from both the giver and the receiver. A person cannot betray another person's True Self for long without causing serious damage to the relationship. In order to grow, the Child Within should *feel* trusted and be able to trust others.

Accomplishment

On a basic level, achieving or accomplishing implies empowerment, "power," "control," or the potential to master, *i.e.*, belief that the person *can* accomplish a task. On a higher level, this means not only completing the task, but also being aware that the task is complete. Perhaps the highest level of accomplishment is the feeling that one *made* a contribution, which offers meaning to the task.

Some people who grew up in troubled or dysfunctional families found it difficult to complete a task or a project or to make decisions. This is because they did not practice doing so with the guidance and support of an important other. By contrast, others from dysfunctional families may be high achievers in some areas, such as education or work, but are repeatedly unable to achieve in other areas, such as intimate relationships.

Altered Consciousness, Enjoyment and Fun

Classifying the alteration of one's state of consciousness as a human need is somewhat controversial. This is because of the folklore that altered consciousness implies using alcohol or other mood-changing drugs (Weil, 1973). Actually, we seem to have an innate — even a biological need — to periodically alter our conscious state, whether it be by daydreaming, laughing, playing sports, concentrating on a project or sleeping. Closely related to this is another need and also an altered state: enjoyment or having fun. Many children from troubled families have difficulty relaxing and having fun. Ability to be spontaneous and to play is a need and a characteristic of our Child Within.

Sexuality

Sexuality is often not mentioned as a human need. Rather than sexual intercourse alone, by sexuality I mean a range of potentials, from feeling good about being a man or a woman, to enjoying various aspects of being sexual, to discovering the man (animus) inside the psyche of the woman or the woman (anima) inside the man.

Many of us who grew up in troubled homes may have difficulty with our sexual identity, functioning or enjoyment. Some of us may have been sexually abused, whether overtly or covertly.

Freedom

Having the freedom to risk, explore and do what is spontaneous and necessary is another human need. Along with this freedom comes responsibility. For example, spontaneity tends to be healthy, whereas impulsivity may work against our best interests.

Nurturing

The next-to-the-last highest order of human needs is nurturing; to provide any or all of the above needs to someone is appropriate in each situation. However, the nurturing person must be able to nurture *and* the person in need must be able to let go, to surrender, in order to *be* nurtured. In my observations of patients, their families, and of other people, this reciprocity is unusual in human interaction.

Unconditional Love

The final need is unconditional love. This is a difficult concept for many to understand. It will be discussed further in Chapter 15.

The Unfulfilled Parent

Rarely does anyone find a mother, other parent figure or close friend who is even *capable* of providing or of helping us to meet all our needs — much less one who delivers them. There is usually no such person available. (In fact, getting pregnant and carrying a child to term is sometimes primarily for the mother's needs.) Thus, in our recovery, we *grieve* over not having had all our needs met as infants, children and even as adults. Grieving over the opposite, *i.e.*, getting things that we didn't want or need, such as child mistreatment or abuse, is also helpful. This grieving process will be described in Chapters 11 and 12.

Many mothers or other parent figures are mentally and emotionally impoverished. A likely reason is that *their* needs were not met as infants, children and/or adults. They are thus so in need that they tend to use others in an unhealthy and inappropriate way to get these needs met. Anyone in their immediate environment, anyone close to or near them, including infants and children, will be unconsciously used (Miller, 1983). In order to survive, the child who cannot develop a strong True Self compensates by developing an exaggerated false or co-dependent self.

At first it may seem inconceivable that a mother would use a vulnerable, helpless newborn infant to get her own needs met. Yet this occurs repeatedly in many troubled or dysfunctional families. Conditions in the child's parents and family that tend to promote such confusion, regression, and misdirection will be described in Chapter 5.

Chapter 5

Parental Conditions that Tend to Stifle the Child Within

How can a mother, other parent figure or, later in life, a close friend be *able to help us meet* many of *our needs?* In general they must have had *their* needs met as children and/or worked through a process as adults of healing their own Child Within and learning to get their needs met.

However, certain conditions may interfere with getting needs met. The more deprived, more severe, or advanced the parent's and family's condition, the less the child's needs tend to be met. These parental conditions are listed in Table 3. The word "parental" means *not only the parent*, but may also include siblings and anyone else, and in the life of an older child and certainly in that of an adult refers to *any close or otherwise influential person.*

Alcoholism and Other Chemical Dependence

Alcoholism or other chemical dependence can be defined as recurring trouble, problems or difficulties associated with drinking or drug use. The trouble may occur in one or more of several areas, including relationships, education, legal, financial, health, spiritual and occupational.

TABLE 3. Parental Conditions Associated with Dynamics of Adult Children of Alcoholics and Other Dys-functional Families

---

Alcoholism

Other Chemical Dependence

Co-Dependence

Chronic Mental Illness and Dysfunctional Physical Illness

Extreme rigidity, punitive, judgmental,
Non-loving, perfectionistic, inadequacy

Child abuse — physical, sexual, mental-emotional, spiritual

Other conditions, *e.g.*, those associated with
post traumatic stress disorder

We know that children of alcoholics (CoAs), and other family members tend to be *unaware* that their parent or other family member is alcoholic or dependent on another drug. Black (1984) estimates that close to half of adult children of alcoholics deny a parental drinking problem. And up to 90% of CoAs who themselves become alcoholic or chemically dependent cannot identify a parental drinking problem. This lack of awareness of the major source of the family chaos results in extensive, destructive and unnecessary acceptance, as well as self blame and guilt among family members.

Any reader who wonders or is concerned about a parent's or another relative's drinking or drug use may find it helpful to answer the following Family Drinking Survey. (If you are no longer living with the family member in question, or if they are deceased, try to answer these questions as though you *were* still living with them. If it is *drug* use about which you have been concerned, substitute "drug use" for "drinking" in the questions.)

Family Drinking Survey

	Yes	No

1. Does someone in your family undergo personality changes when he or she drinks to excess? ___ ___

2. Do you feel that drinking is more important to this person than you are? ___ ___

3. Do you feel sorry for yourself and frequently indulge in self-pity because of what you feel alcohol is doing to your family? ___ ___

4. Has some family member's excessive drinking ruined special occasions? ___ ___

5. Do you find yourself covering up for the consequences of someone else's drinking? ___ ___

6. Have you ever felt guilty, apologetic, or responsible for the drinking of a member of your family? ___ ___

7. Does one of your family member's use of alcohol cause fights and arguments? ___ ___

8. Have you ever tried to fight the drinker by joining in the drinking? ___ ___

9. Do the drinking habits of some family members make you feel depressed or angry? ___ ___

10. Is your family having financial difficulties because of drinking? ___ ___

11. Did you ever feel like you had an unhappy home life because of the drinking of some members of your family? ___ ___

12. Have you ever tried to control the drinker's behavior by hiding the car keys, pouring liquor down the drain, etc.? ___ ___

13. Do you find yourself distracted from your responsibilities because of this person's drinking? ___ ___

14. Do you often worry about a family member's drinking? ___ ___

15. Are holidays more a nightmare than a celebration because of a family member's drinking behavior? ___ ___

16. Are most of your drinking family members' friends heavy drinkers? ___ ___

17. Do you find it necessary to lie to employers, relatives or friends in order to hide your family member's drinking? ___ ___

18. Do you find youself responding differently to members of your family when they are using alcohol? ___ ___

19. Have you ever been embarrassed or felt the need to apologize for the drinker's actions? ___ ___

20. Does some family member's use of alcohol make you fear for your own safety or the safety of other members of your family? ___ ___

	Yes	No

21. Have you ever thought that one of your family members had a drinking problem? ___ ___

22. Have you ever lost sleep because of a family member's drinking? ___ ___

23. Have you ever encouraged one of your family members to stop or cut down on his or her drinking? ___ ___

24. Have you ever threatened to leave home or to leave a family member because of his or her drinking? ___ ___

25. Did a family member ever make promises that he or she did not keep because of drinking? ___ ___

26. Did you ever wish that you could talk to someone who could understand and help the alcohol-related problems of a family member? ___ ___

27. Have you ever felt sick, cried or had a *knot* in your stomach after worrying about a family member's drinking? ___ ___

28. Has a family member ever failed to remember what occurred during a drinking period? ___ ___

29. Does your family member avoid social situations where alcoholic beverages will not be served? ___ ___

30. Does your family member have periods of remorse after drinking occasions and apologize for his or her behavior? ___ ___

31. Please write any symptoms or nervous problems that you have experienced since you have known your heavy drinker. ___ ___

If you answered "Yes" to any 2 of the above questions, there is a good possibility that someone in your family may have a drinking problem.

If you answered "Yes" to 4 or more of the above questions, there is a definite indication that someone in your family does have a drinking problem.

(These survey questions are modified or adapted from the Children of Alcoholics Screening Test (CAST) (Jones, Pilat, 1983), the Howard Family Questionnaire, and the Family Alcohol Quiz from Al-Anon. They are referenced in Whitfield et al, 1986.)

Co-dependence

The next condition is co-dependence, or co-dependency, originally termed "co-alcoholism" in the 1970s. Co-dependence is far more inclusive in the 1980s. Five definitions can be found in Table 4.

Co-dependence is a condition that stifles our True Self, our Child Within. It *results from* and *contributes to* all of the parental conditions in Table 3 above.

We can begin to define co-dependence as *any suffering and/or dysfunction that is associated with or results from focusing on the needs*

TABLE 4. Some Definitions of Co-dependence

---

1) . . . an exaggerated dependent pattern of learned behaviors, beliefs and feelings that make life painful. It is a dependence on people and things outside the self, along with neglect of the self to the point of having little self identity.

(Smalley, S: cited in Wegscheider-Cruse, 1985)

2) . . . preoccupation and extreme dependence (emotionally, socially, and sometimes physically) on a person or object. Eventually, this dependence on another person becomes a pathological condition that affects the co-dependent in all other relationships. This may include . . . all persons who (1) are in a love or marriage relationship with an alcoholic; (2) have one or more alcoholic parents or grandparents; or (3) grew up in an emotionally repressive family . . . It is a primary disease and a disease within every member of an alcoholic family.

(Wegscheider-Cruse, 1985)

3) . . . ill health, maladaptive or problematic behavior that is associated with living with, working with or otherwise being close to a person with alcoholism (other chemical dependence or other chronic impairment). It affects not only individuals, but families, communities, businesses, and other institutions, and even whole societies.

(Whitfield, 1984, 1986)

4) . . . an emotional, psychological, and behavioral pattern of coping that develops as a result of an individual's prolonged exposure to, and practice of, a set of oppressive rules — rules which prevent the open expression of feeling, as well as the direct discussion of personal and interpersonal problems.

(Subby, 1984)

5) . . . a disease that has many forms and expression and that grows out of a disease process that . . . I call the addictive process . . . the addictive process is an unhealthy and abnormal disease process whose assumptions, beliefs, behaviors, and lack of spiritual awareness lead to a process of nonliving which is progressive . . .

(Schaef, 1986)

---

and behavior of others. Co-dependents become so focused upon or preoccupied with important people in their lives that they neglect their True Self. As Schaef (1986) says in her book *Co-Dependence,* it leads to a process of "nonliving," which is progressive.

Endemic in ordinary humankind, co-dependence can mimic, be associated with, and aggravate many conditions. It develops from turning our responsiblity for our life and happiness over to our ego and to other people.

Development of Co-dependence

The genesis of co-dependence begins by the repression of our observations, feelings and reactions. Others — often our parents — and eventually *we* begin to *invalidate* these, our often crucial *internal cues*.

Usually early in this process we begin to deny a family secret or another secret. Because we focus so much on the needs of others, we begin to neglect our own needs, and by so doing we stifle our Child Within.

But we still have feelings, often of hurt. Since we continue to stuff our feelings, we become increasingly tolerant of emotional pain. We often become numb. And because we stuff our feelings, we are unable to grieve our everyday losses to completion.

All of the above blocks our growth and development in the mental, emotional and spiritual aspects of our being. But we have a desire to contact and know our True Self. We learn that "quick fixes" such as compulsive behaviors will allow us to glimpse our True Self and will let off some of the tension. However, if the compulsive behavior is destructive to us or to others, we may feel shame and a resulting lower self-esteem. At this point we may begin to feel more and more out of control and we try to compensate by the need to control even more. We may end up deluded and hurt and often project our pain onto others.

Our tension has now built to such an extent that we may develop stress-related illness manifested by aches and pains and often by dysfunction of one or more body organs. We are now in an advanced state of co-dependence, and may progressively deteriorate so that we experience one or more of: extreme mood swings, difficulty with intimate relationships and chronic unhappiness. For those who are attempting to recover from alcoholism, another chemical dependence, or another condition or illness, this advanced state of co-dependence may seriously interfere.

The development of co-dependence may thus be summarized as follows:

Growth of Co-dependence

1. Invalidation and repression of internal cues, such as our observations, feelings and reactions
2. Neglecting our needs
3. Beginning to stifle our Child Within

4. Denial of a family or other secret
5. Increasing tolerance of and numbness to emotional pain
6. Inability to grieve a loss to completion
7. Blocking of growth (mental, emotional, spiritual)
8. Compulsive behaviors in order to lessen pain and to glimpse our Child Within
9. Progressive shame and loss of self-esteem
10. Feeling out of control. Need to control more
11. Delusion and projection of pain
12. Stress-related illness develops
13. Compulsions worsen
14. Progressive deterioration
   Extreme mood swings
   Difficuty with intimate relationships
   Chronic unhappiness
   Interference with recovery from alcoholism/CD and other conditions

Whether we are an infant or a child growing up with such a co-dependent person, or whether we are an adult living with or close to them, it is highly likely that with our present awareness and coping skills we will be negatively affected. By the process described in the first half of this book, our True Self will be stifled.

The Subtleties of Co-dependence

Co-dependence is one of the most common conditions causing confusion and suffering in the world. It may be subtle in its manifestations, and therefore difficult to identify. The following is a case history of Karen, a 45-year-old woman whose parents were co-dependent and through growing up with them *she* became co-dependent.

"When I heard the characteristics of adult children of alcoholics described, I saw a lot of myself in them. So I looked and looked for an alcoholic in my family background and couldn't find one. I found I had to look deeper as my parents both had a lot of characteristics of co-dependence. My father was also a workaholic. He was such a success. But he gave his time and energy to everyone except his family. He was the mayor of our town, and I felt guilty when I asked him for attention. He just wasn't there for me as a father and to help me when I was growing up. My mother was a compulsive overeater, although I didn't know that at the time. She wasn't the mother I needed either. They both trained me to be a self-sacrificer and a real people-pleaser.

"I married two alcoholic men, and gradually became so focused on them that I neglected my own needs and felt like I was losing my mind. I didn't know how to say 'no' to people. Because my life was going so badly, I tried to correct it the only way I knew how from my past: I worked harder, went back to college, getting into super responsibility and compulsive overactivity. And I neglected my needs even more. I was depressed, and became progressively more depressed, so much so that I took an overdose of sleeping pills. That was my 'bottom.'

"In desperation, I called AA and they told me to go to Al-Anon, which I did. I attended a meeting every day and I loved it. Now it's six years later, and I still attend one meeting a week. I also had 2½ years of group therapy and several months of individual therapy. I found it all very helpful. Looking back, I discovered that not only was my recovery program helpful mentally and emotionally, but it was a great help to me spiritually. I discovered that my biggest problem was with my mother, on whom I had come to depend regarding how I was supposed to feel and how I was supposed to live. I was so sick that I couldn't even feel and live for myself. I had to look to others to see how to feel and live. I was angry at my mother for this and at my father for supporting her for doing so and for his not being there for me when I needed him. And I picked two husbands who unknowingly encouraged me to continue all of these patterns. I'm so glad that I made a recovery."

Karen's story represents some of the subtle manifestations of co-dependence.

Chronic Mental Illness or Disabling Chronic Physical Illness

Chronic mental illness may range from subtle and mild to obvious and disabling. It may include any of the major chronic mental and emotional illnesses listed and described in DSM-III (Diagnostic and Statistical Manual, 3rd edition, of the American Psychiatric Association).

The following is a case history of Barbara, a 56-year-old married woman with four children and a professional career:

"Four years ago I finally went for help. I had been depressed since my early childhood. In therapy I learned that my mother had been chronically depressed most of her life. I remember a time in my mid-twenties when she got me a date with a man with whom *she* was having an affair, while she was still married to and was living with my father. I felt really bad about going out with him. My father had been cold and distant from both me and my mother. Later, when my mother was hospitalized from taking an overdose of sleeping pills, I learned that my father had been impotent for most of their marriage. That was a 'family secret,' of course. I viewed my father's distance and mother's chronic depression as *my fault* as long as I can remember, and I felt a lot of shame and guilt over it. I survived as a child by being obedient, doing well in school and focusing on my mother.

"I took on a caretaker role. As a teenager I went to the library and read everything I could find on psychology in an attempt to cure my mother and father. In my recovery in psychotherapy and in my self-reflection, I learned that I was fused with my mother, that our boundaries were so merged that I literally woke up every morning and didn't know how I felt until I looked at how my mother was feeling. I also learned that my father's coldness and distance had nothing to do with how good a little girl I was or how hard I worked, but it had to do with *him*. I learned that I no longer had to be a victim. Since then I have been feeling better overall, and my life is going better. I continue to work on getting free of my old problems."

By reaching out for help, Barbara came to recognize the damage done to her True Self by growing up in a troubled family, and is now well on her way to recovery.

Extreme Rigidity, Punitiveness, Judgmentalness, Non-Loving, Perfectionism or Inadequacy

Although many people's True Self has been substantially stifled, the exact nature of the "trouble" in their family cannot be easily recognized or labeled. For example, recognizing advanced alcoholism in a family member may be relatively easy because it is so blatant. But recognizing a less obvious condition is more difficult. I have observed and treated hundreds of adult children of alcoholics, other chemical dependents, and co-dependents during long-term recovery. I have also seen several other patients who fit the *description* of CoAs, both by my diagnosis and by their own observations, yet they did not come from an alcoholic, CD or obviously co-dependent family, nor from any of the other more obvious parental conditions listed in Table 3.

Cathy was a 32-year-old woman who grew up in a troubled family. There were no alcoholics in the family, yet she joined and experienced growth in a therapy group for adult children of alcoholics. She represents an increasing number of "adult children of troubled or dysfunctional families," or "adult children of trauma" whose backgrounds, life and suffering are more similar than dissimilar to those of adult children of alcoholics. When she was about midway in her recovery, she wrote the following about her life:

"My parents espoused the 'what will people think' philosophy. In public we really did pull off the 'perfect family' image — we were all very gracious to each other. At home Mom and Dad changed from smiling, chatting, joking, to Dad completely withdrawing physically, verbally, emotionally and Mom yelling for attention.

"I always had a feeling of 'preparing for' or getting ready for something . . . always a flurry of household chores to get through. I felt happiest when I was in the midst of a chore — I had a role. And I learned early to try to bottle tensions by anticipating what needed to be done next — to make it easier for Mom. I consciously worked at not needing anything from anyone again to hopefully cut down on some of my stress.

"Dad was either never home, or sleeping whenever he was at home. He may as well have stayed away. I don't recall any interactions with him other than at a distance — being afraid of him, though he was never verbally or physically abusive. I grew up with a neutral feeling for my Dad, and very strong emotions for Mom: 'taking care' of her by not being a bother, by not giving her any trouble, by anticipating how she would want me to be. This later developed into a strong emotion of hating her for the distance she fostered between Dad and me. For most of my adult life I've wavered between pleasing her and being very rebellious around her wishes for me. Being the fifth of six children, I have a strong memory that Dad didn't know which one I was at times. He was a workaholic outside the home. Mom was very compulsive about things in the home. I am now trying to get in touch with some of my feelings about my dad. I remember quietly living my life, hoping no one saw me, while at the same time craving *anyone's* attention. I was always overweight and always tried to lose the weight, trying to hide because of how I looked.

"I continued my quiet life throughout high school, feeling very protected and safe whenever I was at home. I had a feeling of not wanting to be away from the house. I wasn't like my siblings who went out for sports, drama, speech, etc. This pattern continued in college. I didn't have a safe, protected place to be on campus and my weight became a big problem. I was not developing a direction with my life and attended three colleges, ending up with a two-year degree.

"My adult life became mere survival. I didn't have the capacity to form and maintain relationships. I broke up with any man I was seeing. I moved out on roommates. I left jobs after I started having personality problems with bosses. I kept away from my family on an unconscious level. I became bulimic to control weight gains. I dated men opposite from those Mom would approve. I began smoking and drinking as a sign of my 'independent thinking.'

"I was chronically depressed, isolating and compulsively overeating or dieting. I wanted people to think I had it all together and didn't need anything from anyone, but inside I was so needy that whenever I did have a friend, I expected to be fulfilled from that one person.

"I came into Overeaters Anonymous 3½ years ago, devastated from my binge/purge cycle, and have been abstinent for a year now. I started attending an ACoA therapy group, feeling I fit in this group just like I fit into OA. These people were just like me and I was a lot like them. But I quickly realized this recovery work was too painful to go through. I started ACoA group therapy over a year ago and have attended on a weekly basis.

"For six months I didn't feel any emotions or at least I couldn't identify any. But I was exposed to group members' experiencing feelings about their current issues and identifying and re-experiencing incidents in the past that were too painful to feel before.

"I began to be willing to risk these people knowing me — motivated largely by the desire to stay abstinent from overeating. I began developing a sense of the group representing a safe family in which to develop and to begin to re-experience what I didn't get in my own family. I began to have some honest interactions, even though I was afraid of and not feeling worthy of group time, of undivided attention from the group. But I was slowly getting a growing sense of self-esteem from real, honest interactions in and out of group. I was open to acknowledging that I have feelings, to identifying them, and finally to expressing them to be able to feel my healing. I let go of destructive patterns in relationships and in how I see myself. I was finding inherent worth in my simply 'being.' I talked about what it was like growing up in a home where I felt invisible. Telling the truth as I perceive it has been incredibly freeing for me. Being honest with myself has been the core of recovering — awfully difficult to do since I came to therapy with *no* sense of self. I discovered that for me it takes time to even get an inkling that I have a right to myself. It has taken time and a lot of facing my feelings in constructing a healthy self, one day at a time, through OA and group therapy."

These families — or other family-like environments — for which Cathy's story serves as an example, fit many of the dynamics, described below, of a troubled or dysfunctional family. Some common parental conditions include extreme rigidity, extreme punitiveness, judgmentalness, perfectionism and a cold or nonloving relationship with children and other family members. The parents were inadequate to administer to the mental, emotional and spiritual needs of the child.

These states or conditions are often extremely insidious, subtle, or hidden. They *may be difficult to recognize without some substantial recovery work* in self-help groups, group therapy, individual counseling, or in other forms of introspection by sharing with and listening to trusted others. Outwardly, these families are usually *not* viewed as being troubled or dysfunctional. Indeed, they are often viewed as being "healthy." This category of troubled or dysfunctional family is open for observation, exploration and research.

Child Abuse — Physical, Sexual, Mental-Emotional and/or Spiritual

Child abuse is common in all sorts of troubled families. While severe physical abuse and overt sexual abuse are clearly recognizable as traumatic to infants and children, other forms of child abuse may be more difficult to recognize as being abusive. These may include mild to moderate physical abuse, covert or less obvious sexual abuse, mental and emotional abuse, child neglect, and ignoring or thwarting the child's spirituality or spiritual growth. Examples of covert or more subtle sexual abuse include a parent's flirting, relating sexual experiences, stories or jokes; touching children, adolescents or even adult children on inappropriate parts of their anatomy; and any other unnecessary sexually stimulating behavior. These forms of abuse usually result in deep-seated feelings of intense guilt and shame that are unconsciously carried into adulthood. I will address emotional abuse in more detail later.

Spiritual abuse is likely to be controversial, rarely discussed, yet real. For example, raising a child to be an atheist or cultist may seem like spiritual abuse to some parents, but not to others. More subtle forms taught by some organized religions are the strong teaching of an angry deity, inflicting guilt or shame, or insisting that certain *other* denominations or belief systems are automatically bad or inferior. While the latter may be easily observed in some fundamentalist Christian denominations, they are by no means limited to these, since such characteristics pervade many of our world's religious systems. Indeed, these views are often major factors starting and continuing the many wars that have been fought around the world.

Other conditions stifle our True Self. Some examples may be found under the post-traumatic stress disorder, discussed in Chapter 7.

Some Commonalities

These seven parental conditions often exist in mixtures among troubled families. The stifling of the Child Within, or to use perhaps stronger language — the murder of the child's soul (Schatzman, 1973) — has certain common dynamics within the family. These may include inconsistency, unpredictability, arbitrariness, and chaos (Gravitz, Bowden, 1985; Seixas, Youcha, 1985). Inconsistency and unpredictability tend to repress spontaneity and are in general "crazy making." Combined with arbitrariness, these dynamics may promote lack of trust or fear of abandonment, as well as chronic depression. They result in a chaotic environment. This precludes the development of a safe, secure and reliable foundation from which to learn about ourselves through risk taking.

While many of these characteristics of troubled or dysfunctional families are common, *all may not be present in every troubled family.*

Inconsistent

Many troubled families are inconsistent, and some are not. One way that many troubled families are *consistent* is through consistently *denying the feelings* of many family members and having one or more *family secrets.* Troubled families that are rigid tend to be more consistent and predictable. Because they are excessive, these qualities function to control and shut down family and individual growth.

Unpredictable

Many troubled families are predictable in their unpredictability. That is, family members learn that they can *expect* the unexpected at any time. By contrast, many will know *what* to predict, and even *when* to predict it, although they may not know it consciously or talk about it with others. However, they usually live in chronic fear, as though "walking on eggshells," of when they will suffer their next trauma.

Arbitrary

The arbitrariness means that no matter *who* the family member is or how hard they may try, the troubled person or persons would still mistreat them in the same way. In a family where rules have no rhyme or reason, the child loses trust in the rule setters (the parents) and in him or herself. She is unable to understand the environment. However, while the more rigid families may be less arbitrary, they can still be troubled, painful and dysfunctional and they are often arbitrary about their rigidity.

Chaotic

Chaos may be manifested by any of the following: (1) physical or emotional abuse, which teaches the child shame, guilt and "don't feel;" (2) sexual abuse, which teaches the same, plus distrust and fear of losing control; (3) regular and repeated crises, which teach a crisis orientation to life; (4) predictable closed communications, which teaches "don't talk," "don't be real," and denial; and (5) loss of control, which teaches obsession with being in control, and fusion or loss of boundaries or individuation.

While dysfunctional families tend to be chaotic, in many troubled families chaos is either absent or minimal. Here, chaos is often subtle in its manifestations. Active or overt chaos does not have to be present to stifle our Child Within. Rather, just the *threat* of chaos — whether it be threat of crisis, threat of mistreatment of any form, or threat of seeing another family member mistreated — no matter how simple or transient, can be just as damaging. It does so by instilling fear, which blocks our being real and creative. When we cannot be real and creative, we cannot discover, explore and complete our stories and thereby grow and develop. We cannot have peace.

Even if active chaos occurs only once or twice a year,the threat of its unpredictability, impulsiveness and destructiveness to self and others is enough to chronically destroy peace and serenity.

The family member in the middle of chaos, whether active or threatened, may feel that this is *so routine and so "normal,"* that he or she *does not recognize* it as chaos. This principle is true for all the characteristics in this chapter.

Mistreatment

Child mistreatment in various forms can be *subtle,* although clearly damaging to the growth, development and aliveness of our True Self. Examples are listed in Table 5.

Denial of Feelings and Reality

Troubled families tend to deny feelings, especially the painful feelings of the members. The child — and many of the adults — are not allowed to express feelings, especially so-called "negative" ones such as anger. However, each family usually has at least one

---

TABLE 5. Some Terms for Mental, Emotional, and Spiritual Trauma That May Be Experienced by Children and Adults.

Abandonment
Neglect
Abuse: Physical — spanking, beating, torture, sexual, etc.
     Mental — covert sexual (see below)
     Emotional — (see below)
     Spiritual — (see below and text)

Shaming	Withdrawing/
Humiliating	Withholding love
Degrading	Not taking seriously
Inflicting guilt	Discrediting
Criticizing	Invalidating
Disgracing	Misleading
Joking about	Disapproving
Laughing at	Making light of or minimizing
Teasing	your feelings, wants, or needs
Manipulating	Breaking promises
Deceiving	Raising hopes falsely
Tricking	Responding inconsistently or
Betraying	arbitrarily
Hurting	Making vague demands
Being Cruel	Stifling
Belittling	Saying "you shouldn't . . . feel
Intimidating	such & such, *e.g.*, anger"
Patronizing	Saying "If only . . . *e.g.*, you were
Threatening	better or different" or
Inflicting fear	"You should . . . *e.g.*, be better
Overpowering or bullying	or different" (See also negative
Controlling	messages in Table 6)
Limiting	

---

member, generally the alcoholic or similarly troubled person, who is permitted to express painful feelings openly, especially anger. In such families where anger is chronic and unexpressed directly by members, it often takes other forms, *i.e.*, abuse of self, others, and other anti-social behavior, and various forms of acute and chronic illness, including stress-related illness. What the child sees as reality is denied, and a new model, view of false belief system of reality is assumed as true by each family member. This fantasy often binds the family together in a further dysfunctional way. This denial and the new belief system stifle and retard the child's development and growth in the crucial mental, emotional, and spiritual areas of life (Brown, 1986).

To repeat: while *discovering* some of the conditions described here may feel uncomfortable, it *can start the way out of our suffering and confusion.* We can summarize the common characteristics of troubled or dysfunctional families as including at least one, although usually several, of the following:

- Neglectful
- Mistreating
- Inconsistent
- Unpredictable
- Arbitrary
- Denying

- Having one or more secrets
- Disallowing feelings
- Disallowing other needs
- Rigid (some families)
- Chaotic at times (including crisis orientation)
- Quiet and functional at times

Other characteristics of troubled families may include a variety of neglect and mistreatment. *Reading about and reflecting upon* examples of mistreatment or trauma can help us to find our True Self. Also helpful is *hearing others tell their stories of mistreatment* or trauma. But one of the best ways to begin validating our own mistreatment or trauma is to *tell our* own *story* in the company of people who accept and support us and who will not betray our confidence or reject us. I call such people "safe" or "safe and supportive," and describe these principles in the following chapters.

What other factors or dynamics inhibit our Child Within? In the next chapter I focus on the development of low self-esteem, the shame dynamic and negative rules, negative affirmations or messages.

Chapter 6

The Dynamics of Shame and Low Self-Esteem

Shame or low self-esteem plays a major role in stifling our Child Within. Shame is both a *feeling* or emotion, and an *experience* that happens to the total self, which is our True Self or Child Within (Fischer, 1985; Kaufman, 1980; Kurtz, 1981).

It is also a *dynamic* or *process* that happens to us, especially when we are unaware, and sometimes even when we become aware of the truth about many of the aspects of our shame.

Growing up in a troubled or dysfunctional family is nearly always associated with shame and low self-esteem in all members of that family. Only the manifestations of shame vary among family members. We each adapt to shame in our own way. The major similarity is that nearly everyone will be co-dependent and operates primarily from their false self. We can thus describe the troubled or dysfunctional family as being *shame-based*.

Guilt

People often confuse shame with guilt. While we feel both, there is a difference between them.

Guilt is the uncomfortable or painful feeling that results from *doing* something that violates or breaks a personal standard or value, or from hurting another person, or even from breaking an agreement or a law. Guilt thus concerns our *behavior*, feeling bad about what we have done, or about what we *didn't* do that we were supposed to have done.

Like most feelings, guilt can be a useful emotion to help guide us in our relationships with ourselves and with others. Guilt tells us that our conscience is functioning. People who never experience guilt or remorse after transgressions have difficulty in their lives, and are classically said to have an anti-social personality disorder.

Guilt that is useful and constructive we call "healthy" guilt. We use this kind of guilt to live in society, to resolve our conflicts or difficulties, to correct our mistakes, or to improve our relationships. When guilt is detrimental to our serenity, our peace of mind, and our functioning — including our mental, emotional and spiritual growth — we call it "unhealthy" guilt. People from troubled or dysfunctional homes or environments often have a mixture of healthy and unhealthy guilt. Unhealthy guilt is usually not handled or worked through and lingers on, at times becoming psychologically and emotionally disabling. Our "responsibility" to family overcomes our responsibility to our True Self. There may also be "survivor" guilt, wherein the person feels guilty and unworthy for leaving and abandoning others in a troubled environment or surviving in life after others may have failed (see also Chapter 7).

Guilt can be relieved substantially by recognizing its presence and by then *working it through*. This means that we experience it, and discuss it with trusted and appropriate others. In its simplest resolution, we may apologize to the person whom we may have harmed or deceived, and ask their forgiveness. In its more complex forms, we may have to talk about the guilt in more depth, perhaps in group or in individual therapy.

Guilt is often easier to recognize and resolve than is shame.

Shame

Shame is the uncomfortable or painful feeling that we experience when we realize that a part of us is defective, bad, incomplete, rotten, phoney, inadequate or a failure. In contrast to guilt, where we feel bad from *doing* something wrong, we feel shame from *being* something wrong or bad. Thus guilt seems to be correctable or forgiveable, whereas there seems to be no way out of shame.

Our Child Within or True Self *feels the shame* and *can express it*, in a healthy way, to safe and supportive people. Our co-dependent or false self, on the other hand, pretends not to have the shame, and would never tell anyone about it.

We *all* have shame. Shame is universal to being human. If we do not work through it and then let go of it, shame tends to accumulate and burden us more and more, until we even become its victim.

In addition to feeling defective or inadequate, shame makes us believe that others can see through us, through our facade, into our defectiveness. Shame feels hopeless: that no matter what we do, we cannot correct it (Fischer, 1985; Kaufman, 1980). We feel isolated and lonely with our shame, as though we are the only one who has the feeling.

What is more, we may say, "I'm afraid to tell you about my shame because if I do, you'll think I'm bad, and I can't stand hearing how bad I am. And so not only do I keep it to myself, but I often block it out or pretend that it is not there.

"I may even disguise my shame as if it were some other feeling or action and then *project* that *onto other people.*" Some of these feelings and actions that may mask our shame include:

Anger	Contempt	Neglect or Withdrawal
Resentment	Attack	Abandonment
Rage	Control	Disappointment, and
Blame	Perfectionism	Compulsive Behavior

"And when I feel or act out any of these disguises, it serves a useful purpose to my co-dependent or false self — acting as a *defense* against my *feeling* the shame. But, even though I may defend myself well against my shame, it can still be seen by others; when I hang my head, slump down, avoid eye contact or apologize for having needs and rights. I may even feel somewhat nauseated, cold, withdrawn and alienated (Fischer, 1985). But no matter how well I may defend myself and others against it, my shame will not go away — unless I learn what it is, experience it and share it with safe and supportive others."

An example of the guise that our shame can take happened in group therapy when Jim, a 35-year-old accountant, began to tell the group about his relationship with his father, who lives in another state. "Every time we talk on the phone he tries to judge me. I get so confused that I want to hang up." Jim talked more and interacted with the group, who asked him what feelings were coming up for him right now. He had some difficulty being aware of and identifying his feelings, and made little eye contact with the group. "I'm just confused. I always wanted to be perfect around him. And I never could do it to his satisfaction." He talked further, and the group asked him again what feelings were coming up for him right now. "I feel some fear, some hurt and I guess I'm a little angry." As a group leader, I also asked him if he might be feeling some shame, as though he were somehow an inadequate person. He said "No. Why would you think of that?" I pointed out that his drive to be perfect, his avoidance of eye contact, and the way he described his relationship with his father suggested to me that he was feeling some shame. A tear came to his eye, and he said he would have to think about that.

Where Does
Our Shame Come From?

Our shame seems to come from what we do with the negative messages, negative affirmations, beliefs and rules that we hear as we grow up. We hear these from our parents, parent figures and other people in authority, such as teachers and clergy. These messages basically tell us that we are somehow not all right, not O.K. That our feelings, our needs, our *True Self*, our *Child Within* is not acceptable.

Over and over, we hear messages like "Shame on You!" "You're so bad!" "You're not good enough." We hear them so often, and from people on whom we are so dependent and to whom we are so vulnerable, that we believe them. And so we incorporate or *internalize* them into our very being (Canfield, 1985).

As if that were not enough, the wound is *compounded* by negative rules that stifle and prohibit the otherwise healthy, healing and needed *expression* of our pains (Table 6). Rules like "Don't feel," "Don't cry" and "Children are to be seen and not heard." And so not only do we learn that we are bad, but that we are not to talk openly about any of it.

However, these negative rules are often inconsistently enforced, as described in the previous chapter. The result? Difficulty in trusting rule-makers and authority figures, and feelings of fear, guilt, and more shame. And where do our parents learn these negative messages and rules? Most likely from *their* parents and other authority figures.

TABLE 6. Negative Rules and Negative Messages Commonly Heard in Alcoholic or Other Troubled Families

---

Negative Rules	Negative Messages
Don't express your feelings	Shame on you
Don't get angry	You're not good enough
Don't get upset	I wish I'd never had you
Don't cry	Your needs are not all right
Do as I say, not as I do	with me
Be good, "nice," perfect	Hurry up and grow up
Avoid conflict (or avoid dealing	Be dependent
with conflict)	Be a man
Don't think or talk; just follow	Big boys don't cry
directions	Act like a nice girl (or a lady)
Do well in school	You don't feel that way
Don't ask questions	Don't be like that
Don't betray the family	You're so stupid (or bad, etc.)
Don't discuss the family with out-	You caused it
siders; keep the family secret	You owe it to us
Be seen and not heard!	Of course we love you!
No back talk	I'm sacrificing myself for you
Don't contradict me	How can you do this to me?
Always look good	We won't love you if you . . .
I'm always right, you're always	You're driving me crazy!
wrong	You'll never accomplish anything
Always be in control	It didn't really hurt
Focus on the alcoholic's drinking	You're so selfish
(or troubled person's behavior)	You'll be the death of me yet
Drinking (or other troubled	That's not true
behavior) is not the cause of our	I promise (though breaks it)
problems	You make me sick!
Always maintain the status quo	You're so stupid
Everyone in the family must be an	We wanted a boy/girl
enabler	You _____

The Shame-based Family

When everyone in a dysfunctional family comes from and communicates with others from a base of shame, it may be described as being *shame-based.*

Parents in such a family did not have their needs met as infants and children nor usually as they continue into adulthood. They often use their children to meet many of these unmet needs (Miller, 1981, 83, 84, 86).

Shame-based families often, *though not always,* have a secret. This secret may span all kinds of "shameful" conditions, from family violence to sexual abuse to alcoholism to having been in a concentration camp. Or the secret may be as subtle as a lost job, a lost promotion or a lost relationship. Keeping such secrets disables all members of the family, *whether or not they know* the secret (Fischer, 1985). This is because being secretive prevents the expression of questions, concern and feelings (such as fear, anger, shame and guilt). And the family thus cannot communicate freely. And the Child Within of each family member remains stifled — unable to grow and to develop.

Boundaries

Paradoxically, even though the family may communicate poorly, its members are nonetheless highly connected emotionally and through denial of and loyalty about keeping the secret. Often one or more members are dysfunctional in some capacity so other members take on their roles. Everyone learns to mind everyone else's business one way or another. What results is a group of family members who are *enmeshed*, fused or who have invaded or even overtaken one another's boundaries.

The boundaries of healthy and individuated people schematically look something like the following:

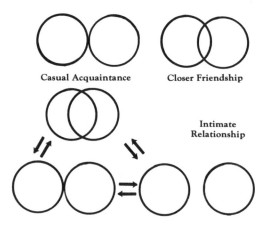

Casual Acquaintance   Closer Friendship

Intimate
Relationship

Healthy relationships are open, flexible, allow the fulfillment of one another's needs and rights, and support the mental, emotional and spiritual growth of each person. While they are often intimate and close, their intensity has a flexible ebb and flow that respects each member's needs and allows each to grow as individuals.

By contrast, the enmeshed or fused relationship may schematically look something like this:

Or in the case of a troubled or dysfunctional family, like this:

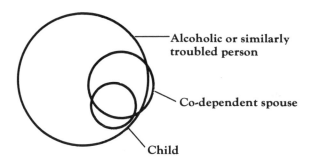

These enmeshed or fused relationships are generally *unhealthy,* closed, rigid, and tend to discourage the fulfillment of one another's needs and rights. They tend *not* to support the mental, emotional and spiritual growth of each person. Little or no ebb and flow of closeness and distance is allowed. The case histories of Karen and Barbara illustrate such unhealthy or fused boundaries.

To survive in such an enmeshed relationship, we generally use several defenses, such as denial (of the secret, our feelings, and our pain), and projection of our pain onto others (attacking, blaming and rejecting) (Course, 1976). However, *when we leave the shame-based relationship*, even though we may have survived and are still surviving, such a shame-based and co-dependent stance of fear, guilt, denial and attacking does not tend to work for us. When we leave an unhealthy relationship and try to use the same ways and defenses in relating that we used to survive in the unhealthy one, *those ways and defenses don't tend to work well in the healthy relationship.*

The co-dependent person is nearly always enmeshed in some way with one or more people. While we are in a co-dependent, shame-based relationship, we may feel like we are losing our minds, going crazy. When we try to test reality, we are unable to trust our senses, our feelings and our reactions.

Compulsive Behavior and the Repetition Compulsion

When we live our life in a shame-based and co-dependent stance, focusing inordinately on others, we naturally feel as though something is missing, that we are somehow incomplete. We are unhappy, tense, distressed, feel bad and/or numb. But to be real seems too threatening to us. We tried being real with others, and too often were rejected or punished for it. And so to be real again, to express our feelings and get our other needs met, seems too scary. Besides, we are not used to doing this. So we defend ourselves against realizing our real needs and feelings (Figure 1).

FIGURE 1. Cycle of Shame and Compulsive Behavior (Modified from Fischer, 1985, with permission)

But our Real or True Self, our Child Within, now alienated and hidden from us, has an innate desire and energy to express itself. Secretly, we want to feel its aliveness and its creativity. Held in for so long, stuck in such an approach-avoidance dilemma, its only way out is through a specific form or negative compulsive behavior that has worked for us in the past, even though we may get only a glimpse of our True Self by doing so. Such compulsive actions range across a wide spectrum of possible behaviors, from heavy use of alcohol or other drugs, to short-term, intense relationships, to trying to control another person. It may involve overeating, oversexing, overworking, overspending or even over-attending self-help group meetings.

This compulsive behavior tends to be negative in some way, such as self-destruction or other-destruction. It may produce a crisis as a side effect or may precipitate a crisis for self and for others. While we can control the behavior to some extent — we have some degree of willpower over it, in that we may even plan it — it often occurs impulsively and automatically, as if by reflex.

When we behave compulsively, we usually get temporary relief from tension, suffering and numbness, even though we might feel some shame about it. And even though of short duration, we feel alive again. However, later we are left feeling shameful and incomplete (Fischer, 1985).

This type of behavior has also been called the *repetition compulsion* (Miller, 1981, 1983). It comes about from unsolved internal conflict that we carry in our unconscious mind, the place within us of which we are not usually aware.

A Way Out

From the recovery experience of hundreds of thousands of people, we know that there is an effective way out of this constricting and binding effect of shame: to tell the story of our suffering to safe and supportive others.

What we expose and share is our Child Within, our True Self, with all of its weaknesses *and* all of its strengths. We cannot heal our shame alone. We need others to help us heal ouselves. They validate our predicaments and our pain, and they accept us as we are. And when we hear others tell their stories and share their shame, we help them to heal *their* shame. Doing so helps *us* as well. By such sharing and listening, we begin to practice the principle of unconditional love.

Such sharing and storytelling is heard and seen countless times each day, whether in self-help groups, group therapy, individual therapy or between intimate friends.

Blocks to Healing

As we begin to heal our shame, we may encounter stumbling blocks *within us* that prevent us from going ahead with our healing. These blocks include: (1) negative *attitudes* that we may have about ourselves; (2) memories of facial expressions or other *images* in people that made us feel shameful in the past that we now see in other people; and (3) the *binding* by shame of some important areas in our lives (Fischer, 1985). These areas may include the following:

1) Feelings
2) Drives (*e.g.*, sexuality, aggression, hunger and the need for intimacy)
3) Needs (see Chapter 4 and Table 2)
4) Thoughts (*e.g.*, especially any "bad" thoughts).

For example, any time that we feel hurt by an authority figure, such as one of our parents, we may feel anger. However, the anger quickly changes into or is covered up by feeling shame. We may also begin to feel fearful and confused. Because all these feelings may begin to feel overwhelming, as though we might lose control, we quickly suppress all of them and become numb. During this, and for several minutes afterward, we can become dysfunctional in varying degrees. This whole process may take just a few seconds, but we may feel as though we are helpless little children again. Such an occurrence has been called *age regression* or reversion to an earlier survival mechanism.

Tom is a 45-year-old attorney and father of two. He tells in group therapy of his discovery of regression to a younger age.

"It took me 45 years to see what happened when my father put me down. Last month when I visited him and my mother, within five minutes of arriving, my father tried to put me down by making a joke of my being an attorney. He said, 'Here comes the shyster lawyer,' and then looked at me, my mother, brother and sister to see if we'd laugh with him. With the help of this group, I've learned how I reacted. I suddenly felt confused, helpless and angry as though I were five years old again. I hung my head and went numb. It was a horrible feeling that I've had hundreds of times growing up, and I still have it when he does that. I also have it around people who try to tease me or judge me. What I'm realizing is that doing that is one of his main ways of handling conflict or tension in our family. He tries to make a joke or tease or put down whomever he is in conflict with. His other way was to *leave* the person, you know, abandon them, so that the conflict was never handled. So I'm practicing recognizing when I age regress and taking deep breaths and walking around to gather my sanity so I can deal with him or people like him. I'm setting limits with my father now when he does that. I'm saying to him, 'I don't like it when you joke about my career like that, and I won't visit you anymore if you keep doing that!' "

We can begin to break free of a shame bind or an age regression by becoming aware of it. When it occurs, we recognize it. And when we recognize it, take *several slow, deep breaths.* Doing this will relieve us of our confusion, numbness and dysfunction, and allow us increased awareness of what is happening, so that we can better take control of ourselves. Instead of being paralyzed, confused and dysfunctional co-dependents, we pull ourselves right back into our True Selves. And we continue to function as our True Selves by *getting up* and *walking around,* and *observing reality* around us. If we are with safe and supportive people, we can then begin to talk about how we feel. We may also *leave* the person who is mistreating us. Even if we don't leave, we can gain comfort by *grasping our car keys,* a symbol of our ability to get away.

We also discover that age regression may even be *advantageous* to us. It tells us immediately that *we are being mistreated!* Or we are being reminded of being mistreated. And when we know that we are being mistreated, we can explore ways of taking action to *remedy the situation* and to *avoid the mistreatment.*

We know that there is a way out. We are beginning to heal our Child Within.

Another symptom may be *avoiding activities associated* with the trauma. A final symptom, not listed in DSM III, is *multiple personalities*. People with multiple personalities often come from highly troubled, stressed or dysfunctional families. Perhaps multiple personalities are often offshoots of the false or co-dependent self, driven, in part, by the energies of the True Self to express itself.

Cermak (1985) suggests that the dynamics of the condition known as "adult child of alcoholic," "CoA syndrome," or other similar terms are a combination of *PTSD* and *co-dependence*. From my experience treating ACoAs and following them in their recovery, as well as treating adult children from *other* troubled or dysfunctional families, I believe that PTSD and co-dependence are likely to be a part of many troubled or dysfunctional families. I further believe that PTSD is but an extreme extension of the broad condition that results from stifling the True Self in any form. When we are not allowed to remember, to express our feelings and to grieve or mourn our losses or traumas, whether real or threatened, through the free expression of our Child Within, we become ill. Thus we can consider viewing a spectrum of unresolved grieving as beginning with mild symptoms or signs of grief to co-dependence to PTSD. A common thread in this spectrum is the blocked expression of our True Self.

Treatment of PTSD consists of long term group therapy with others who suffer from the condition and usually as needed shorter term individual counseling. Many of the treatment principles for healing our Child Within are helpful in treating PTSD.

Cermak (1986) said, "Those therapists who work successfully with this population have learned to honor the client's need to keep a lid on his or her feelings. The most effective therapeutic process involves swinging back and forth between uncovering feelings and covering them again, and it is precisely this ability to modulate their feelings that PTSD clients have lost. (They) must feel secure that their ability to close their emotions down will never be taken away from them, but instead will be honored as an important tool for living. The initial goal of therapy here is to help clients move more freely into their feelings with the assurance that they can find distance from them again if they begin to be overwhelmed. Once children from chemically dependent homes, adult children of alcoholics, and other PTSD clients become confident that you are not going to strip them of their survival mechanisms, they are more likely to allow their feelings to emerge, if only for a moment. And that moment will be a start."

Chapter 7

The Role of Stress: The Post Traumatic Stress Disorder

The post-traumatic stress disorder (PTSD) is a condition that may so affect someone that not only is the Child Within stifled and stunted, but the person often becomes overtly ill from repeated stress and its extreme traumas. The PTSD interacts with the dynamics of co-dependence to such an extent that these two conditions often overlap. What Kritsberg (1986) describes as "chronic shock" among children of alcoholics can be equated to PTSD.

PTSD may occur across a spectrum of manifestations, from fear or anxiety, to depression, to easy irritability, to impulsive or even explosive behavior. To determine whether PTSD is present, the DSM III (1980) suggests that the following four conditions be present.

Recognizable Stressor

The first is the history or the ongoing presence of a recognizable *stressor*. Some examples and degrees of stressors are shown in the DSM III, and are reproduced in a modified form in Table 7 below. While there are countless other examples, I have italicized several of the stressors found among troubled or dysfunctional families.

TABLE 7. Severity Rating of Psychosocial Stressors (from DSM III)

Code Term	Adult Examples	Child/Adolescent Examples
1. None	No apparent psychological stressor	No apparent psychological stressor
2. Minimal	Minor violation of the law; small bank loan	Vacation with family
3. Mild	Argument with neighbor; change in work hours	Change in schoolteacher; new school year
4. Moderate	New career; death of close friend; pregnancy	*Chronic parental fighting; change to new school; illness of close relative; sibling birth*
5. Severe	Serious *illness in self or family*; major financial loss; marital *separation*; birth of child	Death of peer, *divorce* of parents; arrest; hospitalization; *persistent and harsh parental discipline*
6. Extreme	*Death* of close relative; *divorce*	*Death* of parent or sibling; *repeated physical/sexual abuse*
7. Catastrophic	Concentration camp experience; devastating natural diaster	*Multiple family deaths*

From this short list of examples one can see that stressors are commonly found in families and environments that tend to stifle the True Self. However, to determine the presence of PTSD, the type of stressor must be outside the usual range of human experience. Examples of such stressors may include assault, rape, other sexual abuse, serious physical injury, torture, concentration camp experience, floods, earthquakes, military combat and the like. I believe, as do others (Cermak, 1985), that growing up, or living in a seriously troubled or dysfunctional family or similar environment often brings about or is associated with PTSD. The PTSD is said to be more damaging and more difficult to treat if: (1) the traumas occur over a *prolonged* period of time, *e.g.*, longer than six months; and especially so if (2) the traumas are of *human origin*; and if (3) those around the affected person tend to *deny* the existence of the stressor or the stress. All three are present in an actively alcoholic family and in similar troubled families.

Re-experiencing the Trau

The second condition or manifestation is the re-ex the trauma. This may be a history of recurrent : recollections of the trauma, recurrent bad dreams o or sudden symptoms of re-experiencing the traum rapid heart rate, panic and sweating.

Psychic Numbing

An outstanding characteristic of the Child Withi is that it feels and expresses feelings (Chapter 3, co-dependent or false self denies and covers up gen This advanced condition, called psychic numbing, is of PTSD. It may be manifested by a constriction feeling and of expressing feelings, which often result estrangement, withdrawal, isolation or alienation. A festation may be a decreased interest in important li

Describing psychic numbing, Cermak (1986) wr moments of extreme stress, combat soldiers are ofte to act regardless of how they are feeling. Their sur upon their ability to suspend feelings in favor of ta ensure their safety. Unfortunately, the resulting "s one's self and one's experience does not heal easil gradually disappear with the passage of time. Until cess of healing takes place, the individual continues a *constriction of feelings, a decreased ability to recognize* are present, and a persistent *sense of being cut off roundings* (depersonalization). These add up to a con as *psychic numbing.*"

Other Symptoms

Another symptom of PTSD may be *hyperalertnes lance.* The person is so affected and fearful about con that s/he is constantly on the alert for any and all po stressors or dangers, and how to avoid them. Yet a tom is *survivor guilt, i.e.,* guilt felt after escaping or a of the trauma when others are still in the trauma. W guilt is said to lead to the feeling that the survivor ha abandoned others, and often then to chronic depres: that several other factors lead to chronic depression, stifling of the Child Within.

Chapter 8

How Can We Heal Our Child Within?

To rediscover our True or Real Self and heal our Child Within, we can begin a *process* that involves the following four actions.

1) Discover and practice being our *Real Self* or Child Within.
2) Identify our ongoing physical, mental-emotional and spiritual *needs*. Practice *getting* these needs *met* with safe and supportive people.
3) Identify, re-experience and *grieve* the pain of our ungrieved *losses* or *traumas* in the presence of safe and supporting people.
4) Identify and work through our *core issues* (described below).

These actions are closely related, although not listed in any particular order. Working on them, and thereby healing our Child Within, generally occurs in a circular fashion, with work and discovery in one area a link to another area.

Stages in the Process of Recovery

Survival

To get to the point of recovery, we must survive. Survivors are by necessity co-dependents. We use many coping skills and ego defenses to do this. Children of alcoholics and from other troubled or dysfunctional families survive by dodging, hiding, negotiating, taking care of others, pretending, denying and learning and adapting to stay alive using any method that works. They learn other often unhealthy ego defense mechanisms, as described by Anna Freud (1936) and summarized by Vaillant (1977). These include: intellectualization, repression, disassociation, displacement and reaction formation (all of which if overused can be considered to be neurotic) and projection, passive-aggressive behavior, acting out, hypochondriasis, grandiosity and denial (all of which if overused can be considered immature and at times psychotic).

While these defenses are functional in our dysfunctional family, they tend to work poorly for us as adults. When we attempt to participate in a healthy relationship, they tend not to further our best interests. Using them stifles and stunts our Child Within and promotes and reinforces our false or co-dependent self.

Ginny was a 21-year-old woman who grew up in an alcoholic family. At the beginning of her recovery, she wrote the following poem. It exemplifies some of the pain of the survival stage.

Afraid of Night

Like the child waiting in the night
For warm hands and arms to wrap
Themselves around her loneliness:
To spend herself in tears of sudden safety —
And of love.
I, too, in the dark aloneness of self unloved,
Unanchored, abandoned, and denied,
Still summon with silent child cries
the ancient hope —
The old sure magic of wantedness.

The child still lives in me
With that eager hurt of innocence bewildered
And betrayed. Ah, that painful paradox.
To sense the rescue,
And know there is none.
But driven by old dreams, pale yet powerful,
Remembrances of the soft dear touch of love,
I wait.

One waits. One always waits.
It is forgotten — that nameless need
The years have beaten from my wasted heart.
But like some unshaped primeval force,
It beckons, crowds my reality,
Blunts stiff reason.

And I am grotesque with helpless wanting,
Turning my mind inwards, backwards.
Dull, too, is pain with young memories
That weaken and defy,
Submit then die.
I do not live;
I wait in such unhope.

Here Ginny tells us about her pain, numbness, isolation and hopelessness. Yet, she also reflects one ray of potential hope in the line "The child still lives in me."

Part of recovery is to *discover* ourselves, our Child, and how we use these ineffective means of relating to ourselves, to others and to the universe. This can be most productively accomplished during the working stages of recovery.

While it is clear that we are surviving, it is also true that we experience a good deal of pain and suffering. Or we become numb. Or we alternate between suffering and numbness. Slowly we become aware that these very skills and defenses that allowed us to survive as mistreated infants, children and adolescents, do not work well when we try to have healthy, intimate relationships as adults. It is the frustration of this mistreatment, this suffering of co-dependence and this failure in our relationships that do not work for us, that push and at times even force us to begin looking elsewhere than these ineffective methods. That looking elsewhere can trigger our recovery.

Gravitz and Bowden (1985) describe recovery in their ACoA patients as occurring in six stages: (1) Survival; (2) Emergent Awareness; (3) Core Issues; (4) Transformations; (5) Integration; and (6) Genesis (or spirituality). These stages parallel the four stages of life growth and transformation described by Ferguson (1980) and the three stages of the classical mythological hero or heroine's journey as described by Campbell (1946) and by others.

We can clarify and summarize the similarities of each approach as follows.

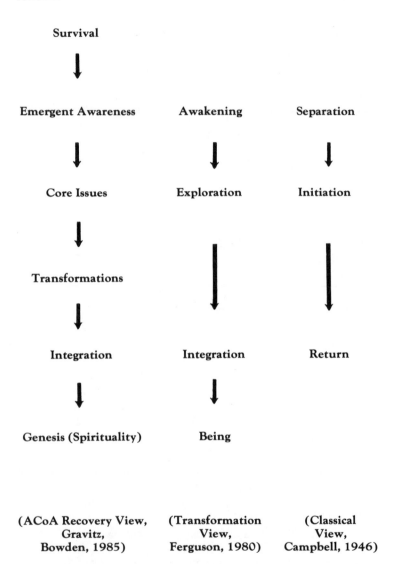

Survival

⬇

Emergent Awareness	**Awakening**	**Separation**

⬇   ⬇   ⬇

Core Issues	**Exploration**	**Initiation**

⬇

Transformations

⬇   ⬇   ⬇

Integration	**Integration**	**Return**

⬇   ⬇

Genesis (Spirituality)	**Being**

(ACoA Recovery View, Gravitz, Bowden, 1985)	**(Transformation View, Ferguson, 1980)**	**(Classical View, Campbell, 1946)**

Each stage is useful in healing our Child Within. Each stage is often recognized only in retrospect. When we are *in* the stage, we do not always realize that we are there. This is one reason why it is helpful to have a sponsor, guide, counselor or therapist during recovery. A therapy group that uses principles of ACoA recovery, described in this book and elsewhere (Gravitz, Bowden, 1985), can be especially helpful.

Awakening (Emergent Awareness)

Awakening is the first glimpse that "things" or "reality" are not what we thought. Awakening is an ongoing process throughout recovery. To begin, we generally require an *entry point* or trigger — anything that shakes up our old understanding or belief system of reality, of the way that we thought things were (Ferguson, 1980; Whitfield, 1985).

Because our True Self is so hidden, and because our false or co-dependent self is so prominent, awakening may not come easily. Nonetheless, it often happens. I have witnessed this process in hundreds of children of trauma. The entry point or trigger may range across a wide spectrum. It may start with hearing or reading someone describe their own recovery or own True Self, or being "sick and tired" of our suffering, or beginning to work seriously on another life problem in counseling or therapy. For others, it may be attending a self-help meeting or an educational experience, reading a book or hearing about it from a friend.

At this time, we often begin to experience confusion, fear, enthusiasm, excitement, sadness, numbness and anger. These mean that we are beginning to *feel* again. We begin to get in touch with who we really are — our Child Within, our Real Self. At this point, some people will give up — will go no further. They find it easier and more "comfortable" to retreat back into their false or co-dependent self (*i.e.*, into a relapse of co-dependence) because these feelings are frightening.

Those who are recovering alcoholic, other drug dependent, or dependent upon other unproductive behavior, such as overeating or compulsive gambling, may begin to experience a relapse. Or they may precipitate another form of shame-based compulsive behavior, such as spending money that they do not have. But this awakening can be an opportunity to take a risk or a plunge to discover our whole self, our aliveness and even eventually our happiness.

Finding Help

At this point it is helpful to find a sponsor, counselor or thera-pist to help us discover and heal our Child Within. The recover-ing person, however, is usually so vulnerable, often related to the confusion, fear and enthusiasm and/or resistance of recovery, that he or she might find a sponsor or clinician who has *not* worked through his or her *own recovery* of *their Child Within*. If that person cannot get his or her own needs met, s/he may use the newly awakened person to meet some of these needs. The result is that the patient, client, student or "pigeon" is traumatized again, resulting in the vicious cycle of unresolved trauma and return to the false self (Miller, 1983; Jacoby, 1984).

Guidelines

The following are guidelines to finding a sponsor, therapist or counselor who will usually tend to be helpful rather than harmful. The person will tend to have:

1) Demonstrable training and experience. For example, a clini-cian or therapist has training and experience in helping people to grow mentally, emotionally and spiritually, as well as being effective in helping with specific problems or conditions, such as being an ACoA or an "AC" (Adult Child of a troubled family)
2) Not dogmatic, rigid or judgmental,
3) No promises of quick fixes or answers,
4) While you sense that they genuinely *care* about you as a human being and about your recovery and growth, they are firm enough to push you to do your own work of recovery,
5) Provide *some* of your needs (listening, mirroring, echoing, safety, respect, understanding and accepting your feelings) during the therapy session,
6) Encourage and help you learn to find ways *outside* the ther-apy session to get your needs met in a healthy way, and
7) They are well progressed in healing their own Child Within.
8) They do not use you to get their needs met (this may be difficult to detect).
9) You feel safe and relatively comfortable with them.

Occasionally a friend during recovery has many of these quali-ties. However, a friend or relative is not forced to listen with full attention, and is generally not trained in helping you with your specific problems. Friends and relatives may want you for *their* needs, sometimes in unhealthy or unconstructive ways. And *some* friends or relatives — usually unconsciously — will, sooner or later, betray you or reject you. You may end up feeling "toxic" or crazy. Being close to these unrecovered people is generally not "safe." Avoid them when possible.

It will probably take some time before you can trust the process of therapy and recovery enough so that you feel OK about taking *risks* to begin exposing your True Self. Give yourself that time. For some, the time needed will be relatively short — a matter of weeks. For others, it may take longer than a year. It is important to share these fears with your therapist and not withhold them. Taking this one step breaks the pattern of denying feelings that you learned as a child.

As you feel a sense of trust, you can begin the former risk of talking about your innermost secrets, fears or concerns. I have described the healing power of telling our story in *Alcoholism and Spirituality,* and others have also described it (Hillman, 1983). Whether in individual or group therapy, it is helpful to talk, even if at first you may stutter or ramble. Feel free to ask your counselor, therapist, group leader or group member for feedback about how you come across. No matter what type of therapy you choose, it is definitely helpful to do some work of recovery on your own, *outside* the session. This can include activities from wondering, considering, questioning and exploring various ideas and possibilities; to keeping a diary or a journal; to telling your dreams to trusted people; to working through conflicts with others.

Eventually, when you talk to others about yourself, it is useful to your recovery that you begin to become clearer and briefer, especially if you are in a therapy group or self-help group.

There is a truism in counseling that people in therapy generally relate and behave in the same or similar ways that they behave outside of therapy. It may be helpful in your recovery to ask your therapist or group how you are doing in this area.

Finally, there is the issue of *transference* in therapy, which includes your feelings and conflicts around your relationship with your counselor, therapist, or group (Jacoby, 1984). Take a risk and express exactly how you feel, even if angry, shameful, guilty or whatever, no matter how unimportant it might seem at first to you. Keep telling yourself that your feelings are OK, despite your fears that they are bad or unjustified.

Once you feel trusting enough so that you can risk self-disclosure in recovery, you are usually ready to begin conscious work on some of your *core issues*.

Chapter 9

Beginning to Deal with Core Issues

An *issue* is any conflict, concern or potential problem, whether conscious or unconscious, that is incomplete for us or needs action or change.

There are at least 14 *core issues* in the recovery of our Child Within that we can work through. Eight of these have been described by clinicians and authors, including Gravitz and Bowden (1985), Cermak and Brown (1982), and Fischer (1985). These core issue are: control, trust, feelings, being over responsible, neglecting our own needs, all-or-none thinking and behaving, high tolerance for inappropriate behavior and low self-esteem. To these I have added being real, grieving our ungrieved losses, fear of abandonment, difficulty resolving conflict, and difficulty giving and receiving love.

As problems, concerns, conflicts or patterns come up in our life, we can bring them up with selected safe and supportive people. At first it may not be clear just which of these core issues —or perhaps more than one of them — is involved for us. Core issues do not present themselves to us as an "issue." Rather, they present at first as problems in everyday life. However, with persistent considering and describing how we feel it will generally become clear which issue or issues are involved. This knowledge will be helpful in gradually getting free of our confusion, discontent, and unconscious negative life patterns (repetition compulsions).

All-Or-None Thinking and Acting

This is the ego defense that therapists call *splitting*. When we think or act this way, we do so at either one extreme of the other. For example, either we love someone completely or we hate them. There is no middle ground. We see the people around us as either good or bad, and not the composite they really are. We judge ourselves equally as harshly. The more we use all-or-none thinking, the more it opens us up to *behaving* in an all-or-none fashion. Both of these actions tend to get us into trouble and to cause us to suffer unnecessarily.

We may become attracted to others who think and behave in an all-or-none fashion. But being around this kind of person tends to result in more trouble and suffering for us.

Table 3 lists types of parental conditions associated with dynamics of ACoAs, and adult children from other dysfunctional families. While all-or-none thinking can occur in any of these parental conditions, it occurs especially often among fundamentalist religious parents. They are often rigid, punitive, judgmental, and perfectionistic. They are often in a shame-based system, which attempts to cover over and even destroy the True Self.

All-or-none thinking is similar to active alcoholism, other chemical dependence, co-dependence or other active addictions and attachments, in that it sharply and unrealistically limits our possibilities and choices. To be so limited makes us feel constricted, and we are unable to be creative and to grow in our day-to-day lives.

In recovery, we begin to learn that most things in our life, *including our recovery*, are not all-or-none, not either-or. Rather, they are *both-and*. They have shades of gray, they are somewhere in the middle, a "3, 4, 5, 6, or 7" and *not* either a "0" or a "10."

Control

Control is perhaps the most dominant issue in our lives. No matter what we think we have to control, whether someone else's behavior, our own behavior or something else, our co-dependent self tends to latch on to this notion and won't let go. The result is often suffering, confusion and frustration.

Ultimately, we cannot control life, so the more that we try to control it, the more out of control we feel because we are focusing so much attention on it. Frequently the person who feels *out* of control is obsessed with the need to be in control.

Another word for control is *attachment*. Wise people have found that attachment or needing to be in control is the basis for suffering. Certainly, suffering is part of life. We all may have to suffer before we can begin to consider our alternatives. Suffering may point out the path toward peace of mind. One alternative that nearly always relieves our suffering is surrender: we surrender our false or co-dependent self, and our attachment to the notion that we can control anything.

We slowly find that one of the most powerful and healing acts is giving up our need to always be in control. This freedom is that of our True Self, our Child Within. In this context, the word "surrender" does not mean to "give up" or to "lie down" in the military sense of losing a war. Rather, we mean that one who surrenders *wins* the struggle of trying to control, and ameliorates most of the resultant needless suffering (Whitfield, 1985). This becomes an ongoing process in life, not a goal to be achieved only once.

Needing to be in "control" is intimately related to and includes several other major life issues: willpower, fear of losing control, dependence/independence, trust, experiencing feelings, especially anger, self-esteem and shame, being spontaneous, self-nurturing, all-or-none and expectations of self and others. Many people have not worked through these important life issues. However, most of the time they believe they have overcome, *i.e.,* controlled these issues and all other life problems. They even believe they can somehow control *life itself.*

It is hard to learn that *life cannot be controlled.* Life's powerful and mysterious process goes on, no matter what we do. Life cannot be controlled because it is far too rich, spontaneous and rambunctious to be fully understood, much less controlled by our thinking, controlling, ego/minds (Cermak, 1985).

At this point we can discover that there is a way out, a way to get free of the suffering associated with our always needing to be in control. The way out is to surrender, and then to become, gradually, a *co-creator* of life. I describe the process of being a co-creator in *Alcoholism and Spirituality.* This is where the spiritual aspect of recovery comes into play as a powerful aid. Attendance at and working 12-step recovery programs such as Al-Anon, Alcoholics Anonymous, Narcotics Anonymous and Overeaters Anonymous is helpful. Other spiritual paths may also be helpful.

We work on our control issues by asking for help from appropriate others and by letting go. When we do this, we begin to discover our True Self, and we begin to feel more alive.

Being Over-Responsible

Many of us who grew up in troubled or dysfunctional families learned to become overly-responsible. That often seemed the only way to avoid many of our painful feelings, such as anger, fear and hurt. It also gave us the illusion of being in control. But what seemed to work then doesn't always work well now.

A 40-year-old patient of mine told me that he always said "yes" to requests at work, and doing that was causing him a lot of suffering. By working on himself for two years in group therapy and by taking a course on assertiveness, he has learned to say "no," and to let others do what he cannot do or does not want to do. He is discovering his True Self, his Child Within.

Instead of being over-responsible, other people may be irresponsible, passive and feel as if they are victims of the world. It is equally helpful for them to work in recovery on these issues; some benefit from assertiveness training.

Neglecting Our Needs

Disowning and neglecting our own needs is intimately related to being over-responsible. Both are part of our false self. It may be useful at this point to review Chapter 4. Some may find it helpful to make a copy of Table 2 which lists some of our human needs and to put this list where we can see it easily and often — perhaps also to carry it with us.

By observing and by working on our recovery we can begin to identify people and places where we can get these needs met in a healthy manner. Gradually, as more and more of our needs are met, we discover a crucial truth: that *we* are the most influential, effective and powerful person who can help us get what we need. The more we realize this, the more we can seek out, ask for and actually realize our needs. As we do so, our Child Within begins to awaken and eventually to flourish, grow and create. Virginia Satir said, "We need to see ourselves as basic miracles and worthy of love."

High Tolerance for Inappropriate Behavior

Children from troubled or dysfunctional families grow up not knowing what is normal, healthy or appropriate. Having no other reference point on which to test reality, they think their family and their life, with its inconsistency, its trauma and its suffering, is "the way it is."

In fact when we assume the role of our false or co-dependent self, which troubled families, friendships and work environments tend to promote, we become fixed in this role — we don't realize there is any other way to be.

In recovery, with appropriate supervision and feedback from skilled and safe others, we slowly learn what is healthy and what is appropriate. Other related issues include: being over-responsible, neglecting our own needs, feelings, boundary issues and shame and low self-esteem.

Tim was a 30-year-old single man who had been in our therapy group for two months. He told us, "When I was a kid, I felt trapped into having to listen to my father's irrational talk and behavior when he was drinking, which was every night and all of most weekends. When I would try to get away from him, I felt so guilty and my mother added to it telling me how selfish I was. Even today as an adult, I let people treat me badly. I let some almost walk all over me. But until I found out about adult children of troubled families and started reading about it and going to meetings, I thought something was wrong with me." Tim is learning about his high tolerance of others' inappropriate behavior and is beginning to get free of this often subtle form of mistreatment.

Fear of Abandonment

Fear of being abandoned goes all the way back to our earliest seconds, minutes and hours of existence. Related to the issue of trust and distrust, it is often exaggerated among children who grew up in troubled or dysfunctional families. Thus, to counter this fear, we often mistrust; we shut out our feelings so we don't feel the hurt.

Some of my patients reported that their parents *threatened* to leave or abandon them as a disciplinary measure when they were infants and young children. This is a cruelty and trauma that may appear benign to some on the surface, although in my opinion it is a covert form of child abuse.

Juan was a 34-year-old divorced man, a successful writer, who grew up in a troubled and dysfunctional family. He told us in group, "I can't remember much about my life before age 5, but at that time my father left me, my mother and my younger sister — out of the blue! He had told my mother he had a job to do out West and would be back. But he didn't tell us kids. And what's more, my mother shipped me off to live with my aunt 600 miles away, without telling me why. I must have been shocked. I denied it all until now. Just in the last few months I've got in touch with my feelings that not only did that SOB abandon me, but my mother rejected me. That must have really hurt that little boy inside of me. I'm just now beginning to get angry about that, too." At a subsequent session, he told us, "One way I learned to handle people abandoning me was not to get too close to them. And with certain women, I'd get very close to *them*, but if any conflict came up for very long, I'd leave them right away. I can view it now that I was abandoning them before they could leave me." Juan continues to work on his feelings of hurt and anger in dealing with this important issue in his recovery — that of abandonment.

Difficulty Handling & Resolving Conflict

Difficulty handling and resolving conflict is a core recovery issue for adult children. It touches upon and interacts with most of the other core issues.

Growing up in a troubled or dysfunctional family, we learn to avoid conflict whenever possible. When conflict occurs, we learn mostly to withdraw from it in some way. Occasionally, we become aggressive, and try to overpower those with whom we are in conflict. When these techniques fail, we may become devious, and attempt to manipulate. In a dysfunctional environment, these methods may help assure our survival. But they do not tend to work in a healthy intimate relationship.

Recovery itself — healing our Child Within — is built on discovering conflict after conflict and then working through each. But the fear and other painful feelings that come up as we get closer to the conflict may be too much for us to experience. Rather than face the pain and the conflict head-on, we may revert to our prior methods. These may include, "I can do it on my own." A problem is that doing it on our own has not worked well for us.

Joanne was a 40-year-old woman who had been in group therapy for adult children of dysfunctional families for seven months. She tried to be the dominant member of the group. But when Ken joined the group, he tried to be assertive with her, and at times was aggressive enough to cause her difficulty and frustration in being as dominant as she had been. After several altercations between Joanne and Ken, Joanne announced that she had decided to leave the group. Upon exploration by the group, their basic conflict was revealed. My co-leader and I said, "Joanne, Ken, and the group are at a crucial point in their recovery. You are right in the middle of an *important* conflict. You have an opportunity here, since this group is a safe place, to work through a core issue for each of you. In the past how have you handled conflict?"

The group members discussed how they often ran away from it, or became aggressive or even manipulative, and that had not worked for them. A group member said to Joanne, "You really do have a chance to work this thing through. I hope you don't leave." She said she would think about it, and the next week she returned and said she had decided to stay in the group.

She told the group that she felt that they didn't listen to her and support her, and that since Ken had joined the group, had felt that more so. More issues were revealed including that she had always had difficulty recognizing her needs and getting them met. She also had always felt unappreciated and unloved by her parents. She, Ken, and the group worked on their conflict, and over the course of several group therapy sessions, have resolved it.

In handling and resolving conflict we first recognize that we are in it. We then take a risk if we feel safe, to disclose our concerns, feelings and needs. By working through conflict, we learn more and more to identify and work through past conflicts and current ones as they come up.

It takes courage to recognize and to work through conflict.

Beginning to Talk About Our Issues

In recovery, we begin to report, from the depths of our True Self, such experiences and fears as that of being abandoned. When we share our feelings, concerns, confusions and conflicts in the company of safe and accepting people, we construct a story that we might not otherwise be able to tell. While it is useful for others to hear our stories, the most useful and healing thing about telling our own story is that *we*, the story-teller, get to *hear our story*. Before we tell it, we don't know exactly how it will come out.

So, no matter which concern, problem or life issue we may want to work on, risking and beginning to talk about it with a safe person or persons is a way out of the unnecessary burden of remaining silent. And when we tell our story from our hearts, bones and guts, from our Real Self, we discover the truth about ourselves. Doing so is healing.

Most often, when core issues and feelings come up for us early in recovery, the co-dependent self actually disguises them into other guises or masks. A task in recovery for us is to learn to recognize issues when they come up. One of the advantages in talking with safe others about our concerns is that doing so helps to expose and clarify our issues.

Other Issues

Of the remaining major or core issues of recovery, I have already discussed that of low self-esteem or shame in Chapter 6. Throughout this book I discuss the issues of being real, grieving and resolving conflict.

Triggering Core Issues

Many situations can trigger our core issues, so that they become activated and begin to enter into our lives more overtly. One situation is an *intimate relationship* — one in which two or more people dare to be their Real Selves with one another. In an intimate relationship we share parts of us that we rarely share with others. Such sharing immediately raises issues like trust, feelings and responsibility. While we have the opportunity for many intimate relationships in recovery, our relationship with our counselor, therapist, therapy group members or sponsor can and does trigger many issues. To deal with these most constructively we can be our Real Self as much as possible. This requires us to surrender, to trust, to risk and to participate. And all of this is potentially frightening.

Other situations that often trigger or precipitate the surfacing of these issues include going through major *life transitions* (Levin, 1980), *demands* on our *performance* at work, home or play, and especially making *visits to our parents* (Gravitz, Bowden, 1985). When the feelings, frustrations and issues surface, we can begin to get free of them if we are real, and if we share our Real Self with safe people whom we can trust.

Chapter 10

Identifying and Experiencing Our Feelings

Becoming aware of our feelings and constructively dealing with them is crucial in the process of healing our Child Within.

People who grew up in troubled or dysfunctional families don't tend to get their needs met. Not getting our needs met hurts. We *feel* the painful feelings. Since the parents and other members of such families tend themselves to be unable to listen to us, to support us, and to nurture, accept, and respect us, we often have no one with whom we can share our feelings. The emotional pain hurts so much that we defend against them by the various unhealthy ego defenses described in Chapter 8, thus shutting the feelings out, away from our awareness. Doing so allows us to survive, although at a price. We become progressively numb. Out of touch. False. Co-dependent.

When we are thus not our Real Self, we do not grow mentally, emotionally, and spiritually. Not only do we feel stifled and unalive, but we also often feel frustrated and confused. We are in a victim stance. We are *unaware* of our total self, and we feel as though others, "the system," and the world are "doing it to us," *i.e.*, we are their victim, at their mercy.

A way out of this victim stance and its suffering is to begin to identify and to experience our feelings. An effective way to facilitate knowing and experiencing our feelings is to *talk* about them with safe and supportive people.

Bill was 36-years-old, successful at work but not in the intimate relationship he wanted. In group therapy one day he said, "I hated my feelings and being always asked to talk about them here. After two years in this group, I'm beginning to see how important they are. And I'm even beginning to *enjoy* them, even though some are painful. Basically, I feel more alive when I feel my feelings."

There is no need for us to know everything about our feelings. All we need to know is that feelings are important, that we each have all of them, and that it is healthy to begin to know them and to talk about them. Our feelings can be our friends. Properly handled, they will not betray us; we will not lose control, be overwhelmed or engulfed — as we fear.

Our feelings are the way we perceive ourselves. They are our reaction to the world around us, the way we sense being alive (Viscott, 1976). Without awareness of our feelings, we have no real awareness of life. They summarize our experience and tell us if it feels good or bad. Feelings are our most helpful link in our relationship with ourselves, others and the world around us.

The Spectrum of Feelings

We have two basic kinds of feelings or emotions — joyful and painful. Joyful feelings make us feel a sense of strength, well being and completion. Painful feelings interfere with our sense of well being, use up our energy and can leave us feeling drained, empty and alone. Yet even though they may be painful, they are telling us something, a message to ourself that something important may be happening, something that may need our attention.

Being aware of our feelings, and feeling them in a natural flow, as they occur spontaneously from minute to minute, day to day, gives us several advantages. Our feelings both warn us and assure us. They act as indicators or gauges of how we are doing at the moment and over a stretch of time. They give us a sense of mastery and aliveness.

Our Real Self feels both joy *and* pain. And it expresses and shares them with appropriate others. However, our false or co-dependent self tends to push us to feel mostly painful feelings and to withhold and not share them.

For simplicity, we can describe these joyful and painful feelings across a spectrum, starting with the most joyous, going through the most painful, and ending with confusion and numbness, as follows:

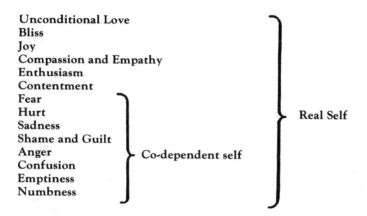

Unconditional Love
Bliss
Joy
Compassion and Empathy
Enthusiasm
Contentment
Fear
Hurt
Sadness
Shame and Guilt
Anger
Confusion
Emptiness
Numbness

Co-dependent self

Real Self

Viewing our feelings in this way, we see that our Real and True Self, our Child Within, is empowered with a wider range of possibilities than we might have believed. The maintenance and growth of our Child Within is associated with what psychotherapists and counselors call a "strong ego," *i.e.*, a flexible and creative ego that can "roll with the punches" of life. By contrast, the co-dependent self tends to be more limited, responding to mostly painful feelings — or no feeling at all, *i.e.*, numbness. Our co-dependent self tends to be associated with a "weak ego," *i.e.*, a less flexible, self-centered (negative or egocentric) and more rigid one. To cover up the pain we use relatively unhealthy ego defenses which give us fewer possibilities and choices in our lives.

Levels of Awareness About Feelings

In order to survive, a person who grew up in or is presently living in a troubled environment tends to be limited to the feeling armamentarium of the co-dependent self. As we begin to explore and become more aware of our feelings, we discover that we can have different levels of awareness about them.

Closed About Our Feelings

When we cannot feel a feeling, we are closed in our ability to use it (Table 8). At that stage not only do we *not know* the feeling, but also we are unable to communicate the condition of our True Self. While we may be talking superficially or even reporting facts, our interpersonal interaction and our ability to experience life and to grow is very low. We can call this stage of growing and sharing our feelings Level One.

Beginning to Explore

At Level Two we can begin to *explore* our feelings. We may be guarded in sharing our newly found feelings, and they may come out in conversation disguised as ideas and opinions rather than actual feelings. At this level interactions with others and our ability to experience life and grow remains low, but it is greater than where we were in Level One. While most people *have* feelings and would often like to express them, most of them do not do so and thus live their lives in a low awareness and sharing of their feelings, limited to functioning in Levels One and Two. This limited use of feelings is what the co-dependent self is accustomed to.

Exploring and Experiencing

As we begin to know our True Self, we begin to explore and to experience our feelings at a deeper or "gut" level. Here we are able to tell others as feelings come up for us how we really feel. By doing so we can have much interpersonal interaction with people who are important to us and can experience our life more. We thereby grow mentally, emotionally and spiritually. When we reach this Third Level of our feelings, we are better able to experience *intimacy* with another.

Sharing Our Feelings

However, sharing our feelings with another is like a two-edged sword. First, we may share them with someone who does not want to listen. They may *themselves* be functioning at Levels One or Two and be incapable of listening. Or they may *appear* to be listening, but are preoccupied with their own agenda, which is entirely different from ours. Or even more painful results could happen. We could share with someone who is not safe and supportive, and we might be rejected for sharing and we may even be betrayed. The difficulty in sharing feelings is shown in the following.

TABLE 8. Levels of Awareness and Communication of Feelings, With Guidelines for Sharing (modified from Dreitlein, 1984)

Our Feeling Condition	Communication	Self Disclosure	Inter-personal Interaction & Ability to Grow	People With Whom To Share Our Feelings	
				Who Are Not Appropriate	Who Are Appropriate
1) Closed	Superficial Conversation, reporting of facts	None	None	Selected people	Most people
2) Beginning to Explore	Ideas and opinions to please others / Obvious facts	Guarded Accidental	Little	People who do not listen	People who listen
3) Exploring & Expressing	Genuine Gut level	Willingness Openness	Much	People who betray or reject us	People who are safe and supportive
4) Open, Expressing Observing	Optimal	Complete when life enhancing	Most	People who betray us or reject us	People who are safe and supportive

Ken was a 34-year-old successful salesman who grew up in a family where his father and brother were actively alcoholic and his mother was co-alcoholic. In his therapy group he spoke of how he had recently set limits on his brother's attending a birthday celebration at Ken's house by asking his brother not to drink or use drugs at the occasion. When asked about how he felt about his brother's potentially disrupting the party since that was his pattern in the past, he told the group that he felt "fine" about it. The group members asked him how he *really* felt and again he said, "Well, fine. But I told you this today to get your feedback." The group continued to ask him how he really felt. Gradually, he realized that he had been blocking and suppressing feeling fear, anger, frustration and confusion, and he told that to the group.

Ken took advantage of being in a therapy group by using them as a mirror, asking them for their feedback. He had been in the group for three months at the time and was beginning to trust the group as being a safe and supportive place and a resource in which he could air his concerns and confusions. He used the group to help him to discover an important part of his True Self.

When we share our feelings, it is most appropriate to do so with safe and supportive people. Early in recovery people who grew up in troubled or dysfunctional families may want so much to share that they get rejected, betrayed or otherwise get into trouble by telling others, indiscriminately, about their feelings. They may find it difficult to learn that it is *not appropriate to share feelings with everyone.*

How do we decide who is safe and who is not? One way is by the technique of share-check-share (Gravitz, Bowden, 1985). When we have a feeling that we want to share, but perhaps aren't sure of who is safe and who is not, we can share just a bit of our feelings with selected people. Then we check their response. If they don't seem to listen or if they try to judge us or if they immediately try to give us advice, we may not wish to share any more feelings with them. If they try to invalidate our feelings, or if they reject us and certainly if they betray us by talking about us, and especially our confidences then they are probably not "safe" to continue sharing with. However, if they *listen,* are supportive and do not react with the above responses, then it may be safe to continue sharing with them. Further clues for "safe" people are those who make *eye contact* with us, tend to appear *sympathetic* and *don't try to* rush in and *change our feelings*. Over the long term someone who is safe will be *consistent* in listening and supporting and *will not betray or reject* us.

Places to practice sharing and checking are a therapy group, a self-help group, with a counselor, therapist, a sponsor or a trusted friend or loved one.

Spontaneous and Observing

As we become more comfortable and able to trust our True Self and others, we can begin selectively to disclose our feelings in a more complete way. As this kind of sharing continues and matures, we can *observe* our feelings more and more (Level Four). As we do so, we discover an empowering and healing principle: *we are not our feelings*. While our feelings are helpful and even crucial to our aliveness and our ability to know and enjoy ourselves and others, we can at the same time simply observe them. Here we are at harmony with our feelings. They do not overtake us or rule us. We are not their victim. This level with our feelings is advanced.

Transforming Our Feelings

Each feeling has an opposite (Table 9). As we become aware of each painful or negative feeling, and as we experience each and then let go of it, we can transform them into joyful feelings. This allows us to experience the gratitude from transforming pain into joy, curse into gift.

Our feelings work in concert with our will and our intellect to help us live and grow. If we deny, distort, repress or suppress them, we only block the flow to their natural conclusion. *Blocked feelings can cause distress and illness.* By contrast when we are aware of experience, share, accept and then let go of our feelings, we tend to be healthier and more able to experience the serenity or inner peace that is our natural condition.

Taking time with our feelings is essential to our growth and happiness. The way out of a painful feeling is "through it."

Our feelings are a vital part of a crucial dynamic in our growth, i.e., our grieving. When we lose something important to us, we have to *grieve* to grow from it.

TABLE 9. Some Feelings and Their Opposites (Compiled in
part from Rose et al., 1972)

Painful	Joyful
Fear	Hope
Anger	Affection
Sadness	Joy
Hate	Love
Loneliness	Community
Hurt	Relief
Boredom	Involvement
Frustration	Contentment
Inferiority	Equality
Suspicion	Trust
Repulsion	Attraction
Shyness	Curiosity
Confusion	Clarity
Rejection	Support
Unfulfillment	Satisfaction
Weakness	Strength
Guilt	Innocence
Shame	Pride
Emptiness	Contentment
	Fulfillment

Chapter 11

The Process of Grieving

A trauma is a *loss*, whether a real loss or a threatened one. We experience a loss when we are deprived of or have to go without something that we have had and valued, something that we needed, wanted or expected.

Minor losses or traumas are so common and subtle that we often do not recognize them as being a loss. Yet all of our losses produce pain or unhappiness: we call this train of feelings grief. We can also call it the *grieving process*. When we allow ourselves to *feel* these painful feelings, and when we *share* the grief with safe and supportive others, we are able to *complete* our grief work and thus be free of it.

To complete our grief work takes time. The bigger the loss, the longer the time generally required. For a minor loss we may complete most of the grieving in a few hours, days or weeks. For a moderate loss this work may require months to a year or longer. And for a major loss the time required for the healthy completion of grieving is usually from two to four years.

Dangers of Unresolved Grief

Unresolved grief festers like a deep wound covered by scar tissue, a pocket of vulnerability ever ready to break out anew (Simos, 1979). When we experience a loss or trauma, it stirs up energy within us that needs to be discharged. When we do not discharge this energy, the stress builds up to a state of chronic distress. Kritsberg (1986) calls it chronic shock. With no release this chronic distress is stored within us as discomfort or tension that may at first be difficult for us to recognize. We may feel it or experience it through a wide range of manifestations, such as chronic anxiety, tension, fear or nervousness, anger or resentment, sadness, emptiness, unfulfillment, confusion, guilt, shame or, as is common among many who grew up in a troubled family, as a feeling of numbness or "no feelings at all." These feelings may come and go in the same person. There may also be difficulty sleeping, aches, pains and other somatic complaints, and full blown mental, emotional or physical illness may result. In short, we pay a price when we do not grieve in a complete and healthy way.

If we suffered losses in our childhood for which we were not allowed to grieve, we may grow up carrying several of the above conditions into and throughout our adulthood. We may also develop a tendency toward self-destructive or other-destructive behaviors. These destructive behaviors may cause us and others unhappiness, get us into trouble and can cause us crisis after crisis. When these destructive behaviors are repeated, they may be called a "repetition compulsion." It is as if we have an unconscious drive or compulsion to keep repeating one or more of these behaviors, even though they are not usually in our best interest.

Children who grew up in a troubled or dysfunctional family suffer numerous losses over which they are often unable to grieve in a complete way. The many negative messages that they get when they try to grieve set up a major block: *not feeling* and *not talking* about it (See also Table 6 in Chapter 6). When these rules and patterns that are learned as children and adolescents continue into adulthood, they are difficult to change. Yet in healing our Child Within, in finding, nurturing and being our True Self, we can change these ineffective behaviors and occurrences. In doing so we begin to break free of the bonds of our repeated and unnecessary confusion and suffering. We first have to *identify* our losses or traumas. Then we can begin to *re-experience* them, going *through* our grief work and *completing* it, rather than trying to go around it or trying to avoid it as we have been doing up until now.

Beginning to Grieve

We can begin our grief work through any of several possible ways. Some of these ways include beginning to:

1) Identify our losses
2) Identify our needs (Table 2)
3) Identify our feelings and share them (Chapter 10)
4) Work on core issues, (Chapter 9) and
5) Work a recovery program.

Identifying Our Losses

Identifying a loss may be difficult, especially one that we may have "stuffed," repressed or suppressed. Identifying a loss that happened long ago may be even more difficult. While talking about our suffering and our concerns may be helpful, simple talking or "talk therapy" may not be enough to activate feelings or grief around ungrieved losses.

That is why *experiential* therapy or techniques can be so helpful in activating and facilitating grief work. Experiential techniques, such as group therapy, risking one's real concerns or family sculpture, allow a focus and a spontaneity that taps into the unconscious processes which otherwise may remain hidden from our ordinary awareness. Only an estimated 12% of our life and our knowledge is in our *conscious* awareness, in contrast to 88% that is in our *unconscious* awareness. These experiential techniques are helpful not only in identifying, but also in doing our actual work of grieving.

The following are examples of some experiential techniques that may be used to heal our Child Within through grieving our un-grieved losses or traumas.

1) Risking and sharing, especially feelings, with safe and supportive people.
2) Storytelling (telling our own story, including risking, and sharing)
3) Working through transference (what we project or "transfer" onto others, and vice versa for them)
4) Psychodrama, Reconstruction, Gestalt Therapy, Family Sculpture
5) Hypnosis and related techniques
6) Attending Self-Help Meetings
7) Working the 12 Steps (of Al-Anon, AA, NA, OA, etc.)
8) Group Therapy (usually a safe and supportive place to practice many of these experiential techniques)

9) Couples Therapy or Family Therapy
10) Guided Imagery
11) Breathwork
12) Affirmations
13) Dream Analysis
14) Art, Movement and Play Therapy
15) Active Imagination and Using Intuition
16) Meditation and Prayer
17) Therapeutic Bodywork
18) Keeping a journal or diary

These experiential techniques should be used in the context of a full recovery program, ideally under the guidance of a therapist or counselor who knows principles of healing our Child Within.

To help further in identifying our losses, especially our un-grieved ones, I have compiled some examples of losses (Table 10). This list can be supplemented by also re-reading or referring to Table 5, which describes some terms for various losses or traumas that we may have experienced as children and as adults.

TABLE 10. Some Examples of Loss (Compiled from Simos, 1979)

Important Person — Close or Meaningful Relationships
Separation, divorce, rejection, desertion, abandonment, death, abortion, stillbirth, illness, geographic move, children leaving home, etc.

Part of Ourself
Body image, illness, accident, loss of function, loss of control, self-esteem, independence, ego, expectations, lifestyle; needs; culture-shock; job, etc., change.

Childhood
Healthy parenting, getting needs met, healthy development (through stages), transitional objects (blanket, soft toy, etc.), gain *or* loss of siblings or other family members, body changes (*e.g.*, in adolescence, middle age and older age). Threats of loss; separation or divorce.

Adult Developmental
Transitions, including mid-life.

External Objects
Money, property, necessities (keys, wallet, etc.), car, sentimental objects, collections.

A loss may be sudden, gradual or prolonged. It can be partial, complete or uncertain or unending. It can occur singly or be multiple and cumulative. Always personal, it may also be symbolic.

Since loss is such a universal experience because we encounter it daily, we easily and often overlook it. Yet it always carries with it a threat to our self-esteem. Indeed, loss occurs any time we suffer a blow to our self-esteem (Simos, 1979).

While loss often occurs separately and discreetly, its resulting grief brings up prior un-grieved losses that have been stored in our unconscious. An ungrieved loss remains forever alive in our unconscious, which has no sense of time. Thus past losses or even a reminder of the loss, just as current losses or the memory of past losses, evoke fear of further loss in the future (Simos, 1979).

In summary,

> Past losses and separations
>   have an impact on
>   current losses, separations and attachments.
> And all of these factors bear on
>   fear of future losses and
>   our capacity to make future attachments.
>   (Simos, 1979)
> Identifying an ungrieved loss is
>   a beginning of getting free
>   of its often painful hold on us.

Because loss can be such an overwhelming event in recovery from alcoholism and co-alcoholism or co-dependence, I have considered 10 losses to be grieved in these conditions as further examples for people, who may have been affected, to continue to identify some of their ungrieved losses (Table 11).

Stages of Grief

Acute grief tends to follow an approximate course, beginning with shock, anxiety and anger, progressing through pain and despair, and ending on either a positive or a negative note, depending on the conditions around the loss and the person's opportunity to grieve it (Bowlby, 1980).

TABLE 11. Some Losses in Alcoholism, Chemical Dependence, Co-dependence, and Adult Children of Alcoholics and other Troubled or Dysfunctional Families, and Their Estimated Severity of Impact On the Need to Grieve Them

Loss	Estimated Severity or Impact of Loss in:		
	Alcoholism/ Chem. Dependence	Co-Dependence	Adult Child
1) Expectations; hopes, beliefs	++	++	++
2) Self-esteem	++	+-++	+-++
3) Parts of self (other than self-esteem)	+	+	+
4) Lifestyle	++	++	++
5) Instant altered state of consciousness and/or pain relief (the alcohol or the drug or the adrenalin high)	+++	++	++
6) Past unexperienced relationships			
7) Past incompleted developmental stages	++	+++	+++
8) Past ungrieved losses & traumas			
9) Changes in current relationships			
10) Threats of future loss	++	++	+-++

KEY: + = some, ++ = moderate, +++ = much

(estimated severity or impact of loss in each condition)

These stages or phases may be further described by breaking them down into more detailed components.

Stage 1. Shock, alarm and denial.

Stage 2. Acute grief, consisting of:

> Continuing, intermittent, and lessening denial.
> Physical and psychological pain and distress.
> Contradictory pulls, emotions and impulses.
> Searching behavior composed of:
>> preoccupation with thoughts of the loss, a compulsion to speak of the loss, a compulsion to retrieve that which was lost, a sense of waiting for something to happen, aimless wandering and restlessness, a feeling of being lost, of not knowing what to do, inability to initiate any activity, a feeling that time is suspended, a feeling of disorganization and a feeling that life can never be worthwhile again, confusion and feelings that things are not real, fear that all the above indicate mental illness.
>
> Crying, anger, guilt, shame.
> Identifying with traits, values, symptoms, tastes or characteristics of the lost person.
> Regression or return to behaviors and feelings of an earlier age or connected with a previous loss or reactions thereto.
> Helplessness and depression, hope or hopelessness, relief.
> Decrease in pain and increasing capacity to cope over time.
> A compulsion to find meaning in the loss.
> Beginning thoughts of a new life without the lost object.

Stage 3. Integration of the loss and grief.

> If the outcome is favorable:
>> Acceptance of the reality of the loss and return to physical and psychological well-being, diminished frequency and intensity of crying, restored self-esteem, focus on the present and future, ability to enjoy life again, pleasure at awareness of growth from the experience, reorganization of a new identity with restitution for the loss and loss remembered with poignancy and caring instead of pain.

If the outcome is unfavorable:
> Acceptance of the reality of the loss with lingering sense of depression and physical aches and pains, diminished sense of self-esteem, reorganization of a new identity with constriction of personality and involvement and vulnerability to other separations and losses (Simos, 1979).

Breaking these stages down into components is helpful to our conceptualizing and understanding the grief process. However, these components are not discrete and sequential — *i.e.*, they do not follow each other in any prescribed order. Rather, they tend to overlap and to move around the various areas and manifestations listed above.

Dana was a 28-year-old woman who grew up in an abusive and actively alcoholic family. In her late teens she became alcoholic, and four years ago, at age 24, she stopped drinking and began treatment for her alcoholism. She had been in our therapy group for adult children of alcoholics and other troubled families for about two years, making noticeable progress. When she broke up with her boyfriend, she told the group, "I'm hurting so bad. I'm down to my last hurt, this emptiness is so bad. I broke up with my boyfriend two weeks ago. This week I started crying and just couldn't stop. I'm realizing that breaking up is not all that is making me feel so bad. It is my loss of that little girl inside of me. I've been going home every night and crying myself to sleep." Here she cries, and takes a long pause. "I just can't believe that that little girl was treated as bad as she was. But it's true."

In beginning to grieve over one loss — the relationship with her boyfriend — she triggered her unfinished grieving over another loss — the mistreatment and abuse of her Child Within. This is an example of how grieving is not always as simple as it might first appear. Of course, Dana had been grieving the loss of her Child Within for a long time, although it was in an incomplete way: through the repetition compulsion of going out with men who mistreated her, by not trusting her sponsor in A.A. and not trusting the therapy group for nearly the first year of her joining it. But gradually she began to risk and to tell her true story little by little. She is now beginning to break free of the shackles of her co-dependent self and her repetition compulsion and to heal her Child Within.

To work through the pain of our grieving, we *experience our feelings as they come up* for us, without trying to change them. Grief is thus *active* work. It is mental and emotional labor, exhaustive and exhausting (Simos, 1979). It is so painful that we often try to avoid the pain around it. Some ways that we may try to avoid grieving include:

- Continuing to deny the loss
- Intellectualizing about it
- Stuffing our feelings
- Macho mentality (I'm strong; I can handle it by myself)
- Using alcohol or other drugs
- Prolonged attempt to get the lost object back

Even though we may get temporary relief by such methods, not feeling our grief only prolongs our pain. Overall, we consume as much energy in avoiding grieving as we would if we went ahead and grieved our loss or trauma. When we *feel* something, we decrease its power over us.

In healing our Child Within we may discover that we have been avoiding grief work over losses or traumas that happened a long time ago. Yet we suffered much and long through our inability to grieve. For some of us it may now be time to begin to work through and to complete our grieving.

There are many possible ways to facilitate feeling and experience our feelings as they come up for us. I listed several possible experiential techniques under "Identifying Our Losses" above. The first two of these are among the most readily available for us: Risking, sharing and telling our story with safe and supportive people.

Chapter 12

Continuing to Grieve: Risking, Sharing and Telling Our Story

Risking

When we risk, we expose our*self*, our Child Within, our True Self. We take a chance and we become vulnerable. When we do this, two extreme outcomes may emerge — acceptance or rejection. Whatever we may decide to risk about ourself, another may accept, reject — or they may react somewhere in between.

Many of us may have been so wounded from risking — whether in our childhood, adolescence, adulthood or all three — that we are usually reluctant or unable to risk and share our Real Self with others. Yet we are caught in a dilemma: when we hold in our feelings, thoughts, concerns and creativities, our Child Within becomes stifled and we feel bad, we hurt. Our held-in energy may build up so much that the only way we can handle it is to let it out to *someone.* This is the predicament that many of us who grew up in troubled families encounter. And because of a number of factors, such as our seeking approval, validation, excitement and intimacy, we may select someone who is *not safe* and supportive. Indeed, they may reject us or betray us in some way, which may just confirm our reluctance to risk. So we hold in all our feelings again and the cycle continues. Yet to heal our Child Within we have to share it with others. So where do we start?

Rather than hold it in and then let it out impulsively or haphazardly, we can begin a step at a time. Find someone who we know is safe and supportive, such as a trusted friend, a counselor or therapist, a therapy group or a sponsor. Begin by risking one little thing. Follow the share-check-share guideline described above (Gravitz, Bowden, 1985). If it works, share some more.

Risking and sharing involves several other core issues, including trust, control, feelings, fear of abandonment, all-or-none thinking and behaving, and high tolerance for inappropriate behavior. When any of these issues come up, it can be useful to consider, and even to begin talking about it with safe people.

As we risk, we can eventually begin to tell our story.

Telling Our Story

Telling our story is a powerful act in discovering and healing our Child Within. It is a foundation of recovery in self-help groups, group therapy and individual psychotherapy and counseling. I describe some of the dynamics of story telling in *Alcoholism and Spirituality*.

Each of our stories when complete contains three basic parts: separation, initiation and return (Campbell, 1949). Twelve-Step self-help groups describe their stories as "What we were like," "What happened" and "What we are like now." People in group therapy may call it risking, sharing, participating and "working" in group. In individual counseling or psychotherapy we may describe it by similar names, and psychoanalysts may call it "free association, working through transference and through unsolved internal conflict." Among close friends, we may call it "baring our souls" or "having a heart-to-heart talk."

In sharing and telling our story we can be aware that gossip and wallowing in our pain are usually counterproductive to healing. This is in part because gossip tends to be attacking rather than self-disclosing and it is generally incomplete, following the victim stance or cycle. Wallowing in our pain is continuing to express our suffering beyond a reasonable duration for healthy grieving. There is a danger here that may be observed in some self-help meetings: When a person tries to tell a painful story that has no apparent or immediate resolution, the other members may unknowingly label it as "self-pity" or a "pity party." In this case, while self-help meetings are generally safe and supportive, the bereaved may wish to look elsewhere to express their pain.

Simos (1979) said, "Grief work must be shared. In sharing, however, there must be no impatience, censure or boredom with the repetition, because repetition is necessary for catharsis and internalization and eventual unconscious acceptance of the reality of the loss. The bereaved are sensitive to the feelings of others and will not only refrain from revealing feelings to those they consider unequal to the burden of sharing the grief but may even try to comfort the helpers" (*i.e.*, the listener).

Our story does not have to be a classical "drunkalog" or long in length. In telling our story we talk about what is important, meaningful, confusing, conflicting or painful in our life. We risk, share, interact, discover and more. And by so doing we heal ourselves. While we can listen to the stories of others, and they can listen to ours, perhaps the most healing feature is that *we*, the story teller, *get to hear our own story*. While we may have an idea about what our story is whenever we tell it, it usually comes out different from what we initially thought.

I have illustrated our story in Figure 2. Starting at the point on the circle called "contentment," we can forget that we are *in* our story. Eventually in our day-to-day life we experience a loss, whether it be a real or a threatened loss. The stage is now set for both grieving and growing. In Figure 2 I have summarized most of the initial pain of our grieving as *hurt*. And when we feel hurt, we tend to get angry.

At this crucial point we have a *possibility* of becoming *aware* that we have experienced a loss or are suffering an upset. And here we can choose to make a *commitment to facing our suffering and grieving head-on*. We can call this cycle of our story a "completed" one or the "hero/heroine's journey." *Or* we may remain *unaware* of the possibility of working through our suffering around our loss or upset. We may then begin to build up a resentment and/or to blame ourselves, which eventually leads to stress-related illness, and to more prolonged suffering than if we had worked through our upset and our grieving in the first place. We can call this cycle the "victim cycle" or the "martyr/victim stance."

If we commit to work through our pain and grieving, we then begin to share, ventilate, participate and to experience our suffering. We may need to tell our story in such a fashion several times

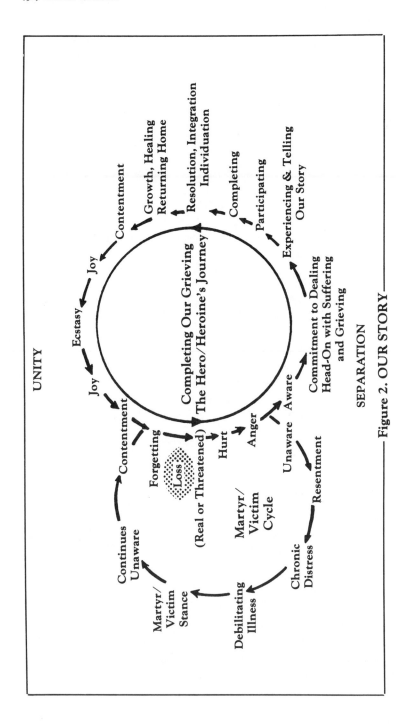

Figure 2. OUR STORY

periodically over a period of several hours, days, weeks or even months — in order to finally complete our story. We may also have to consider it in other ways, mull it over, dream about it and even tell it again.

While this has been painful for us, we are now complete with our upset or conflict. We are free of its pain. Our conflict is now resolved and integrated. We have learned from it. We have healed our Child Within and have grown. And we can settle back to our natural state of our Child Within, which is contentment, joy and creativity.

However, to begin to tell our story may be difficult. And when we tell it, it may be difficult to express our feelings around it. And among our most difficult feelings to recognize and to express is anger.

Anger is a major component in grieving and in healing our Child Within.

Getting Angry

Anger is one of the most common and most important of our feelings. Like other feelings it is an indicator to us of what we might need to attend to.

People who grew up in a troubled family often do not realize how angry they are nor how useful it can be for them to recognize and express their anger even if their traumas or mistreatments happened many years ago. When they were children and adolescents, they were often repeatedly mistreated. This mistreatment may be subtle. As discussed above in Chapter 9, under "High Tolerance for Inappropriate Behavior," children and adults *often do not realize that they have been mistreated.* Having no other reference point from which to test reality, they think that how they were treated — and often how they still *are* being treated — is somehow appropriate or OK. Or if not appropriate, that they somehow *deserve* to be so mistreated.

Through *hearing the stories of others* in recovery, we slowly learn what mistreatment, abuse or neglect actually is. In recovery in group therapy or individual therapy, becoming and being aware of our feelings and *expressing* them, is shown to be a *distinct advantage in eventually living a successful and peaceful life.* As we discover our mistreatment, we can begin the necessary and freeing process of grieving and mourning. Becoming aware of our anger and expressing it is a major part of that grieving process.

One of the few deficiencies of some of the 12-step self-help groups is their hidden fear of feelings and emotions, especially painful ones. There is even a saying "H.A.L.T." — don't get too hungry, angry, lonely or tired. The newly-recovering person can just as easily take this to mean "hold in your feelings" as to its more accurate meaning "take better care of yourself so that you can help prevent being overwhelmed by these feelings."

Many people in recovery are afraid to express their anger. They are often fearful that they might lose control if they really get angry. Then they might hurt someone, hurt themself or something else bad might happen. Were they to pursue it, they would often discover that their anger is not a superficial upset, but is actually *rage*. And to be enraged is scary. It is normal to be scared over becoming aware of and fully expressing our anger.

Often accompanying being angry, there may be somatic or nervous symptoms, such as trembling, shaking, panic, loss of appetite and even a feeling of excitement. It can be freeing to get in touch with and express our anger. Yet in a troubled family or environment, the healthy awareness and expression of feelings is discouraged and may even be forbidden.

As a child, adolescent or adult, we experience a loss or a trauma, whether real or threatened, and from that experience respond, most basically, with fear and hurt. However, *in an environment where feelings can't be expressed,* we feel as though we *caused* the loss or trauma. We feel shame and guilt. But neither can these be openly expressed. So we may then feel even more angry, and if we try to express that, we are squelched again. With repeated stuffing or repressing of such feelings, our Child Within is left feeling confused, sad, shameful and empty. As these painful feelings build and accumulate, they begin to become intolerable. With repeatedly nowhere to ventilate them, our only choice seems to be to block them all out as best we can, *i.e.,* to become numb.

We actually have four *additional* choices, which we may learn as we grow older: (1) to hold it in until it gets unbearable; (2) unable to let it out, we get physically or emotionally sick, and/or we may "blow up;" (3) to blot the pain out with alcohol or other drugs; or (4) to express the pain and work through it with safe and supportive people.

Blotting the pain out with alcohol or other drugs, whether prescribed by a physician or self-administered, is generally not effective for long and may be dangerous, in part for the child of an alcoholic parent or grandparent, because of the tendency of alcoholism and other chemical dependence to be familial or possibly inherited in such families. Doing so also blocks or delays healthy grief resolution. A problem is that many of us have reached out for help with our pain and we have been *given* drugs to lessen the pain, rather than be counseled that we are in the process of grieving and encouraged to work through it.

Holding the pain in until it gets so unbearable that we blow up is an outlet that is often modeled in troubled families. While doing so is probably more effective than drinking or using drugs to handle it, or than becoming numb, it is not nearly so effective as ventilating the pain *when it happens or "comes up"* with a person who is safe and supportive.

Protecting Our Parents: A Block to Grieving

In the previous chapter I listed six ways that we may use to avoid the pain of grieving: denying our loss, intellectualizing about it, stuffing our feelings, being macho, using alcohol or drugs and prolonged attempting to get the lost object back.

In further discussing anger we can now describe another block to grieving: that of protecting our parents and other parent and authority figures from our anger. Before and during grieving and discovering our Child Within we may sense, believe or fear that if we get angry at our parents, it will not be appropriate or that something bad will happen. This belief and fear is perhaps related in part to the "don't talk, don't trust, don't feel" rule described in this book and elsewhere (Black, 1981). In Table 12 below I list nine ways that we, as children and adults, tend to protect our parents from our anger.

The first way is by outright denial. We may say something, like, "Oh, my childhood was fine" or "I had a normal childhood." Such was their trauma, that many adult children of alcoholic, troubled or dysfunctional families cannot remember up to 75% of their childhood experiences. In my clinical experience, however, when working in recovery, most adult children *are* able to work through the denial and to gradually uncover their ungrieved losses or traumas and work through them. Hearing others' stories in

TABLE 12. Answers, Approaches and Strategies often Used to Protect the Parents (and thus Block Healing)

Category	Frequently Heard
1) Outright denial	"My childhood was fine."
2) Appeasing; "Yes, but . . .", detaching from the feelings	"It happened but . . . they (my parents) did their best."
3) Viewing pain of the trauma as a fantasy	"It really didn't happen that way."
4) Fourth Commandment	"God will be angry at me. It just isn't right."
5) Unconscious fear of rejection	"If I express my rage, they won't love me."
6) Fear of the unknown	"Something really bad will happen. I might hurt someone, or they might hurt me."
7) Accepting the blame	"I'm the bad one."
8) Forgiving the parents	"I'll just forgive them" or "I've already forgiven them."
9) Attacking the person who suggests doing recovery work	"You're bad for suggesting that I express my hurt and rage or that my parents could have been bad."

group therapy, ACoA self-help meetings and elsewhere is a help in identifying and recognizing what happened to us. We can then begin to mobilize our grieving, which includes getting angry.

The second answer, approach or strategy to protect our parents is by taking an appeasing attitude, such as "Yes, my childhood may have been somewhat bad, but my parents did the best they could." Doing so is often a way that we detach from our feelings. Assuming such a "why bother" stance prevents us from beginning necessary grief work in getting free of our suffering.

Next is viewing the pain of our loss or trauma as being a fantasy. This one is commonly projected onto us if we do our recovery work in psychoanalysis or psychoanalytically oriented psychotherapy. The analyst or therapist may suggest or imply that if a trauma happened to us, we never can remember it the way that it *actually* happened, with the implication that it is a fantasy. Compounding the wound, this once again invalidates the pain of our Child Within (Miller, 1983). We end up concluding something like, "It really didn't happen that way."

In whatever method of therapy or counseling, we may be exhorted to admit that our fears are now groundless, our defiance no longer necessary and our need for acceptance long since met by the therapist, counselor or general therapy group. We may also be told that while we may hate our parents, we also love them, and that what they did wrong was done only out of love. Miller (1984) says "The adult patient knows all this, but he is glad to hear it again because it helps him once more to deny, pacify and control the Child Within him who has just begun to cry. In this way, the therapist or the group or he himself will talk the child out of his 'silly' feelings because they are no longer appropriate in the present situation (although still intense); a process that could have produced positive results — namely, the awakening and maturation of the child's true self — will be undermined by a method of treatment that refuses to offer support to the angry child." To get free from mistreatment, we usually need to get angry.

The next way of blocking our anger is by the Fourth Commandment, which says "Honor thy father and thy mother, that their days may be long upon the land which the Lord thy God giveth thee." (King James Version, Exodus 20:12). It is difficult to decipher or interpret exactly what the word "honor" means in this context. Over the centuries, however, it has been interpreted by most *parents* to mean "no back talk" and other such stifling messages to the child. We may conclude from this Fourth Commandment something like, "God will be angry at me if I get angry at my parents. It just isn't right," or "I will be an evil or a bad person if I get angry at them." Most organized religions around the world have similar exhortations, which tend to stifle our Child Within and our ability to be real and to work through our losses in a healthy manner.

A fifth way of avoiding our anger and grieving by protecting our parents is by being afraid of rejection by them. We may consider, think or say something like, "If I express my rage, they won't love me," or "They may treat me like a bad little boy or girl again." This is a genuine fear that needs to be expressed when it comes into our awareness.

A sixth way is by being fearful of the unknown, or fear of expressing feelings. We may say or think, "Something really bad will happen. I might hurt someone or they might hurt me." This is another genuine fear that we may need to express in recovery. We may also accept the blame onto ourself, saying, "I'm the bad one."

Many people avoid their anger and their grief by simply "forgiving" their parents. Assuming that forgiving is an easy act, they may say "I'll just forgive them." Or often more stifling to their True Self, "I've *already* forgiven them." However, most people who say this have not forgiven completely, since forgiving is a *process* that is analogous to, if not in large part *identical* to the grieving process.

A final method of protecting our parents is by attacking the person who suggests that we may need to do recovery work, especially any work that might involve expressing anger at or blaming our parents. We may say or think something like, "You are bad for suggesting such a thing!" or "How dare you suggest that my parents could have been bad?"

In one or in a combination of these ways, we protect our parents from our hurt, anger and rage. And by doing so, we stifle our True Self and block our ability to recover from needless suffering. However, *we are now armed with the knowledge of just these blocks.* Now, when we start to use them in any way — perhaps unknowingly, to impede our grieving — we can begin to *let go* of them when we are ready.

Expressing Our Anger

We are learning that in healing our Child Within it is *appropriate* and *healthy* to become aware of and to express our anger. But how can we express it? And to whom?

It is becoming clearer to us that there are some people who are able to listen to our anger and to help us process it. These are the safe and supportive people that I have mentioned — therapists, counselors, sponsors, therapy groups and self-help group members and trusted friends. By contrast, there are other people who, for one reason or another, are unable to tolerate or to hear our anger. These may include our parents and others who may in some way remind us of our parents. If we express ourself the way we need to *directly* to the parent or other person in question, it is *unlikely* that a healing experience will be completed. The person may well not understand what we are trying to say or what we are trying to do. Or they may reject our expression, our offering to risk ourself, and we may feel confused, hurt and powerless again. While it would be cathartic if we could ventilate our anger to these people, doing so would likely not be in our best interest. And it might even end up being self-destructive. Because they have not healed *their* Child Within, they are generally unable to be a part of the safe and supportive healing of another. However, we *can* learn to *set limits* with these people, so that they do not continue to mistreat us. *We set limits both with firmness and with love.* We do so not with aggressiveness, but with *assertiveness.*

While it is usually helpful to eventually make peace with and, through the grieving and the forgiveness process, to forgive our parents and others who have mistreated us, it is important that we not rush or hasten this process. There are some therapists and counselors who may insist on making reconciliation with our parents an immediate or ultimate goal of therapy. But premature efforts in this direction can actually block discovering and healing our Child Within. It is best that we take our time.

And even if we work for a long time to discover and heal our Child Within, we may not be able to heal our differences with our parents. We come to the realization that we cannot fix them. They are the way they are, and nothing that we can do will change that. And so we let go.

For some people whose parents or others — such as an actively alcoholic, violent or otherwise abusing person — are "toxic" to them, it may be helpful to separate from them for a few months to a year or more. Such a separation or "detoxification" period provides a space and a peace that will allow us to begin to discover and heal our Child Within.

Further Principles

The more we were hurt by the lost object or event that we grieve, the more anger we generally have. And even if we had a fairly healthy relationship with the lost object, we can still get angry at it for leaving us helpless and deprived. We may also get angry at others, including those we believe in some way were responsible for the loss, and at anyone who is not suffering as we are. Finally, we may get angry at having to pay for counseling and even at our counselors or therapists for pushing us to do our grief work.

Eventually after we have worked through our anger and the rest of our grieving, we let go of our anger and our suffering. We come to a point where we have had enough.

Chapter 13

Transforming

Through various ways, including being real, self-reflection, therapy groups, self-help groups and counseling, many people are transforming their lives to become more free, whole and fulfilling.

Transformation is a changing of form, a forming over, a restructuring. Ultimately it is a shift from living our life to get somewhere to living our life as an expression of our being (Leonard, 1973; Erhard, 1984). When we transform, we transform our awareness or consciousness. We switch from one domain of reality and being to another. Through such change, we grow and transcend to higher, more empowering, more peaceful and more creative levels of being. At the same time that we experience more personal power and more possibility and choice, we also begin to take more responsibility for making our lives work (Whitfield, 1985).

In the transforming stage of recovery we work to *expose* the vulnerable parts of our Child Within and almost paradoxically at the same time claim the powe. that is inherently there, *within* our Child (George, Richo, 1986). We transform the burdensome and often dysfunctional parts of our lives into positive and more functional ones. For example, when we identify, work through and change our core issues, we may make some of the following transformations.

Recovery Issues	Transformed Into
Grieving past and current issues	Grieving current losses
Difficulty being real	Being real
Neglecting our needs	Getting our needs met
Being over-responsible for others	Being responsible for self, with clear boundaries
Low self-esteem	Improved self-esteem
Control	Taking responsibility, while letting go of control
All-or-none functioning	Freedom from all-or-none
Difficulty trusting	Trusting appropriately
Difficulty with feeling	Observing and using our feelings
High tolerance for inappropriate behavior	Knowing what is appropriate, and if not, asking a safe person
Fear of abandonment	Freedom from fear of abandonment
Difficulty resolving conflict	Resolving conflict
Difficulty giving and receiving love	Loving self, others and Higher Power

Making such changes in our lives may not come easily. We have to work at it by risking and telling our story to close people who are safe and supportive. However, when we transform, we generally don't just one day feel a low self-esteem, wish we felt better about ourself, and the next morning awaken with a healthy self-esteem. Rather, there are specific steps in this kind of life-changing work.

Working on a *single* issue at a time that either *concerns* us or *comes up* for us is usually the most helpful way to go about the process of transforming. Gravitz and Bowden call it "chunking it down," or breaking down a possible plan or solution to a problem into step-by-step or component parts. I have given a beginning outline form to some of these steps in Table 13 below.

Joan was a 33-year-old woman who worked on the core issue of neglecting her own needs. As long as she could remember she nearly always focused on other people's needs and would end up neglecting her own. She had developed a pattern of finding particularly needy people to associate with which helped her to focus on others. In group therapy she said, "Before now I never really knew

TABLE 13. Some Steps in Transforming and Integrating Recovery Issues in Healing Our Child Within

Recovery Issues	Early	Middle	Advanced	Recovered
1) Grieving	Identifying our Losses	Learning to grieve	Grieving	Grieving current losses
2) Being real	Identifying our real self	Practicing being real		Being real
3) Neglecting our own needs	Realizing we have needs	Identifying our needs	Beginning to get our needs met	Getting our needs met
4) Being over-responsible for others, etc.	Identifying boundaries	Clarifying boundaries	Learning to set limits	Being responsible for self, with clear boundaries
5) Low self-esteem	Identifying	Sharing	Affirming	Improved self-esteem
6) Control	Identifying	Beginning to let go	Taking responsibility	Taking responsibility while letting go
7) All-or-None	Recognizing and identifying	Learning both/and choices	Getting free	Freedom from all-or-none choices
8) Trust	Realizing trusting can be helpful	Trusting selectively	Learning to trust safe people	Trusting appropriately
9) Feeling	Recognizing and identifying	Experiencing	Using	Observing and using feelings
10) High tolerance for inappropriate behavior	Questioning what is appropriate and what is not	Learning what is appropriate and what is not	Learning to set limits	Knowing what is appropriate, or if not, asking a safe person.
11) Fear of abandonment	Realizing we were abandoned or neglected	Talking about it	Grieving our abandonment	Freedom from fear of abandonment
12) Difficulty handling and resolving conflict	Recognizing and risking	Practicing expressing feelings	Resolving conflicts	Working through current conflicts
13/14) Difficulty giving and receiving love	Defining love	Practicing love	Forgiving and refining	Loving self, others, and Higher Power

I *had* any needs. The whole idea was foreign to me. But I'm beginning to see that I do. The need I'm working on right now is being able to relax and have fun. Even that word 'working' may sound funny for this issue, but that's what I'm doing. I'm always so serious that I don't even know what it's like to let my hair down and have fun. I guess I never got to learn to *be* a kid and to *play* as a kid. I was always super-responsible. My counselor gave an assignment to take 30 minutes each day and just play, relax or have fun. And she wants me to do that for an hour each day on Saturdays and Sundays. I'm not sure I can do it. But I'm trying it. After doing it the first day, I forgot about it for the next five days. So I see that I'm resisting it."

By breaking down the process of getting needs met into first *realizing* that we *have* needs, and then beginning to *identify* them, we begin to work through the issue of our neglecting our needs. Acomplishing *just these steps* regarding our needs *may take several months* or longer. Eventually we will begin to get one or more of our needs met on a regular basis. With increasing awareness and continued work upon and attention to our needs, we will have transformed our lives so that we now actually *get* our needs met most of the time.

After becoming aware of core issues, we now work with them. Becoming more aware, we act on what we experience, calling things for what they are. We learn to *respect our own internal monitoring system* — our *senses and reactions*. Ignoring or neglecting this crucial part of us is now a thing of the past. We are open to our feelings, senses and reactions, all an important part of our Real Self.

When useful, we call into play the share-check-share process, described above (Gravitz, Bowden, 1985). We share a little at a time, and check the other person's response. If we sense that they are listening, have heard us, are being real with us and are not going to reject or betray us, we can choose to share some more, and then check again.

Breaking Free of Being a Victim

We also begin to see the connections between what we are doing now and what happened to us when we were little. As we share our story, we begin to break free of being a victim or a martyr, of the repetition compulsion.

Richard was a 42-year-old father of three and a successful businessman. He had married two women who turned out to be alcoholic; he was presently in divorce proceedings with his second wife.

"Until now I never realized what I was doing. With the help of counseling and this group I've discovered a pattern that ended up hurting me. My mother was alcoholic, although I never could see that, and certainly couldn't admit it until now. I guess I never could help her, so I had to go out — without realizing what I was doing — and find a woman who I *could* help. But I couldn't help either of them either. Al-Anon and this therapy group helped me to see that. My eyes are now open to try to avoid my previous mistakes. I feel a lot better about myself now."

Richard has transformed a part of his life, the way he creates and lives his story. What he has transformed are his awareness, actions and behaviors. The life story that he creates and tells now is one of a recovering or former martyr/victim who unknowingly acted in a repetition compulsion to a person who is more aware of what he is feeling and doing. As we have described in "Telling Our Story," he is now out of the martyr/victim cycle and into the hero/heroine's journey. The following are some further descriptions of some of the components in these two ends of the spectrum of transformation.

Martyr/Victim Cycle	Hero/Heroine's Journey
False self	True Self
Self-contraction	Self-expansion
There and then	Here and now
Unfinished business	Finished and finishing business
Few personal rights	Many personal rights
Stagnation, regression	Growth
Sharing little	Sharing as appropriate
Same story	Growing story
Repetition compulsion	Telling our story
Impulsive and compulsive	Spontaneous and flowing
Most is unconscious	Much is conscious
Unaware stuckness	Progressively aware becoming and being

Matyr/Victim (cont'd)	Hero/Heroine (cont'd)
Unfocused	Focused
Not working a recovery program	Working a recovery program
Less open to input from others	Open to input from safe others
Varying degrees of "dry drunk"	Working through pain and appreciating joy
Doing it "on my own"	Co-creatorship
Often grandiose	Humble yet confident
Fewer possibilities and choices	More possibilities and choices
"Unhappy dream"	"Happy dream" (A Course in Miracles)
Excludes Higher Power	Includes Higher Power
Illness	Health
Curse	Gift

In recovery our core issues resurface many times, and we continue to become more aware of them as we work on them. As we do so, we discover that these issues are not isolated but often *interact with* or even *include* other issues. For example, the issue of trust often interacts with or even includes the issues of all-or-none, control and low self-esteem.

Letting Go, Turning It Over and the Forgiveness Process

Many people get into a 12-step or other program of recovery from alcoholism, chemical dependence, co-dependence, overeating, neurosis or other form of suffering, and after attending the program regularly and even working it for two or more years, are still not happy. Often when someone brings up family issues, or anger, or confusion in a standard 12-step meeting, the group will avoid it or someone will say "Why don't you just turn it over," as if it were easy to get free of our confusion and suffering immediately. ("Turn it over" generally means to turn our upset or resentment over to a Higher Power.)

But we cannot "turn it over" without first knowing *what* it is that we want to turn over. We then need to know it *more deeply*, i.e., by beginning to *experience* our conflicts, feelings and frustrations. We experience *not intellectually*, but deeply, in our "heart, guts and bones," the core or fiber of our being. We can facilitate our experiencing by risking, talking and telling our story with safe others. The deeper our wound or trauma, whether it be past or present, the more often we will likely have to tell our story and grieve over not getting what we wanted. This may take weeks, months or at times even years of talking about and expressing our feelings around our wounds.

Only after we have so identified and experienced our pain to completion are we authentically able to begin considering the *possibility* that we may have a *choice*. The choice is to continue suffering or to stop suffering over whatever we have discovered is of concern for us, whatever has upset us. If we choose to stop suffering and feel authentically ready to do so, we can then *let go* of it. It is usually only at that point that we are able to "turn it over," and really be free of it. This entire step-by-step process, can be called several names, including the forgiveness process, the detachment process, turning it over, decathexis, or simply "letting go."

We can summarize this process as follows.

1. Become *aware* of our upset or concern,
2. *Experience* it, including telling our story about it,
3. Consider the *possibility* that we may have a *choice* to stop suffering over it, and then
4. *Let go* of it.

In healing our Child Within, we work through this process of identifying or becoming aware, experiencing and then letting go. Since most of us have suffered a large number of ungrieved losses in our lives, working through them may take a long time. This is a test of our *patience*. In jest some have referred to the prayer for patience: "God (Allah, etc.) please give me patience and give it to me now!"

Being Assertive

During the transformation stage in healing our Child Within we begin to become aware of the difference between being assertive and being aggressive. Being aggressive is usually some sort of attacking behavior — whether verbal, non-verbal or physical, that *may* get us what we want, but usually leaves us and the other person feeling upset or bad about the encounter. By contrast, being assertive usually helps us get what we want or need, but *without* leaving us or another feeling upset or bad. In fact, a major indicator of whether we have been assertive is that we and the other person feel okay or even good about the interaction.

Many children growing up in troubled or dysfunctional families learn how to be either aggressive or manipulative *or* to sit back or withdraw. They don't get what they want or need. They almost never see assertiveness being modeled, are rarely taught to be assertive and thus grow up to be adults who operate by being either aggressive, and/or manipulative or passive, "people pleasers," or a combination of these.

Being assertive will usually get us what we want or need. But learning to do so usually takes practice. Some places to practice being assertive are with the safe and supportive people referred to throughout this book. An especially productive place to practice being assertive is in a therapy group. Some people, however, will also find the need for taking an assertiveness training course. Such courses are usually available in most communities and are inexpensive.

Bob was a 30-year-old accountant who joined a therapy group for adult children of troubled families. He was shy, withdrawn and quiet in the group. Try as he would, he couldn't seem to get his points across in group. A fellow group member who had taken assertiveness training suggested that he also take such a course. After doing so, Bob became much more active and expressive both in and outside of group. "I learned to speak up for myself," he told us. "Now when something is bothering me or when I want something, I speak up for it. It's still difficult for me but now I make myself speak up after I've thought about what I want to say. And each time I'm successful at being assertive, it gets a little easier."

When we transform and become assertive, others around us may be taken aback by our change. They may even try to make us think there is something wrong with *us* because we have changed.

Joe was a 52-year-old married man, father of one, who grew up in a troubled family that had much difficulty with boundaries — always minding one another's business. He spent his childhood and much of his adult life confused, resentful and sad. In his recovery he began to become more assertive and self-assured. "Recently when I stood up to my father when he mistreated me, I felt so good about it, because I was assertive. Later my mother who saw me be assertive with him told my sister, 'I don't know what's wrong with your brother Joe lately. He's so different. I wonder what's *wrong* with him?' . . . as though I'm crazy or something. If I didn't have my wife and this group to talk to, I'd probably believe her, that maybe there *is* something wrong with me, that maybe I'm going crazy. But I know I'm not — in fact, I'm getting *healthier.*"

Joe is having an experience that is common to many people who are in recovery and who are healing their Child Within. Oftentimes people who either knew us in the past or know us now may notice a change in us. Depending on where we are in our recovery, they may notice that particular change in us, and become afraid that *they* might have to change some day. Fear may build up in them to such an extent that to handle it they often dump it in some way onto others, often onto the person who they saw changing. It can be threatening to some people to see others change.

A Personal "Bill of Rights"

By the transformation stage we begin to discover that we have rights as individual human beings. As children and even as adults we may have been treated by others as though we had few or no rights. We may have ourselves come to believe that we had no rights. And we may be living our lives now as though we have none.

As we recover and heal our Child Within, we can put together our personal "bill of rights." As part of the therapy groups that I have facilitated, I have asked the group members to consider what rights they have, to write them out and to share them with the group. The following is a compilation of rights that several groups have created.

Personal Bill of Rights

1. I have numerous choices in my life beyond mere survival.
2. I have a right to discover and know my Child Within.
3. I have a right to grieve over what I didn't get that I needed or what I got that I didn't need or want.
4. I have a right to follow my own values and standards.
5. I have a right to recognize and accept my own value system as appropriate.

6. I have a right to say *no* to anything when I feel I am not ready, it is unsafe or violates my values.
7. I have a right to dignity and respect.
8. I have a right to make decisions.

9. I have a right to determine and honor my own priorities.
10. I have the right to have my needs and wants respected by others.
11. I have the right to terminate conversations with people who make me feel put down and humiliated.
12. I have the right *not* to be responsible for others' behavior, actions, feelings or problems.
13. I have a right to make mistakes and not have to be perfect.
14. I have a right to expect honesty from others.
15. I have a right to all of my feelings.

16. I have a right to be angry at someone I love.
17. I have a right to be uniquely me, without feeling I'm not good enough.
18. I have a right to feel scared and to say "I'm afraid."
19. I have the right to experience and then let go of fear, guilt and shame.
20. I have a right to make decisions based on my feelings, my judgment or any reason that I chose.
21. I have a right to change my mind at any time.
22. I have the right to be happy.
23. I have a right to stability — *i.e.*, "roots" and stable healthy relationships of my choice.
24. I have the right to my own personal space and time needs.
25. There is no need to smile when I cry.
26. It is OK to be relaxed, playful and frivolous.
27. I have the right to be flexible and be comfortable with doing so.
28. I have the right to change and grow.
29. I have the right to be open to improve communication skills so that I may be understood.
30. I have a right to make friends and be comfortable around people.
31. I have a right to be in a non-abusive environment.
32. I can be healthier than those around me.
33. I can take care of myself, no matter what.
34. I have the right to grieve over actual or threatened losses.
35. I have the right to trust others who earn my trust.

36. I have the right to forgive others and to forgive myself.

37. I have the right to give and to receive unconditional love.

You may wish to consider whether you have any of these rights. My belief is that every human being has every one of these rights and more.

As we transform we begin to integrate our transformations into our lives.

Chapter 14

Integrating

As we transform we begin to integrate and to *apply* our transformation to our daily life. To integrate means to make whole from separate parts. Healing means moving toward wholeness or integrating — "coming into order," (Epstein, 1986). Healing and integration are the opposite of the confusion and chaos of the past. From all of our recovery work we now use what we have learned and integrated for the good in our life.

By this stage we have progressively less and less confusion and difficulty in using what we have worked through and learned. Now we simply *do* what needs to be done, almost as though by reflex.

At the integration stage we are just who we are and have no need to apologize to anyone for being ourself. Now we can relax, play and have fun without guilt. At the same time we have learned to set limits where doing so is appropriate for our needs. We know and act upon our rights.

We can begin to put a picture together that may help to clarify this *process* of healing our Child Within (Figure 3). In this illustration, we see that recovery is not a static happening or an event. It doesn't simply happen to us and then we start enjoying life. Recovery is not an all-or-none issue. Rather, it is an ongoing *process* that continues in the here and now, over a multiplicity of here and nows.

In our recovery we don't awaken just once. We awaken numerous times. And we don't risk and tell our story just once. We tell

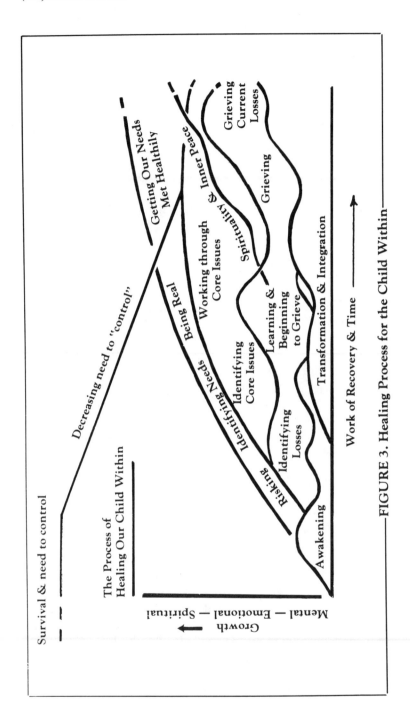

FIGURE 3. Healing Process for the Child Within

it many times as we occasionally suffer, we grow and, on balance, enjoy our lives.

We begin to identify our losses from our past and present and grieve them as they come up. And as core issues surface for us, we talk about them and work through them. As we identify our issues, we may notice that two come up for us often: all-or-none thinking and behaving, and control. Depending on the number and severity of our ungrieved losses, we may have had to use this kind of thinking and behaving to survive (see top left of Figure 3). Being a small child there were few other ways. But now in the transformation and integration stage we begin to get free of their hold on us. And as we do so, we notice that our need to control is gradually decreasing.

We begin to identify our needs and search out ways to get them met in a healthy manner. And we begin to practice being real by being our Real Self.

Healing our Child Within does not usually occur in a linear fashion, as may be suggested by the sequences in Figure 3. Rather, it tends to occur in waves or in a circular fashion and then in a spiral one, as does our story. Each time we complete and integrate a story, *i.e.*, that particular "episode" of our life story, we are then free to create a newer, bigger and more truthful or honest story. Part of this truth and honesty has to do with our being real, who we really are. As we progress and grow in life, we then compile and create bigger and bigger stories and then integrate each into our life (see Figure 4).

In our healing, integration and growth, there will often be what feels like regression, slipping backwards or backsliding. Everything we seemed to have gained, we may feel like we have lost. We may end up feeling confused, hopeless and in pain. This is a crucial point in our story and in our life. This is an opportunity for us to learn something important about our Child Within. Because if we stay with our feelings and our experiences of the Present Moment, the Now, even though all may seem lost, we will likely once again discover that the way out of our pain is *through* it. We help ourself go through it by being in it and telling our story about it to trusted others.

It will also be helpful for us to experience the pain and the joy in solitude. It can be at this time of solitude that we consider that there is something in life more powerful than we. While doing so can be difficult, if we dare, we can even go inward in a state of

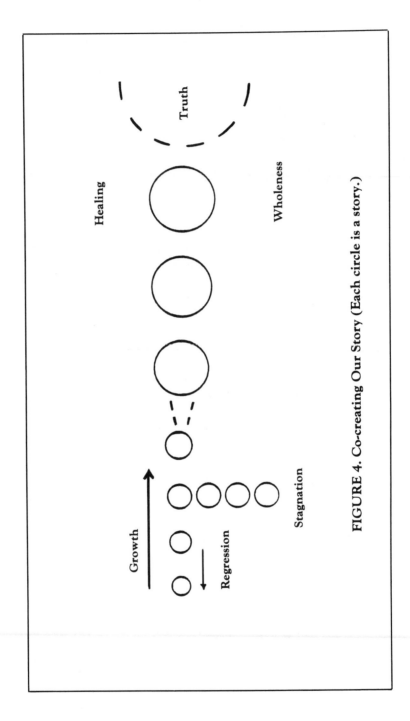

FIGURE 4. Co-creating Our Story (Each circle is a story.)

humility and surrender, and ask such a question as "If there is a God or a Higher Power out there, please help me."

By now this process is familiar to us. Not only is it our story but it is identifying a loss whenever one may come up for us and then grieving it. As we so grieve our loss and tell our story, we can consider a new possibility — that we can take a step back from it at times and *observe* it. When we step back even farther and observe, we begin to see a pattern of *many* stories, ebbing and flowing, growing and regressing, but in an ever upward and expanding direction overall (Figure 5). Given time, this is our recovery and our growth.

When we were children, to survive in our particular environment we had to tolerate being mistreated. Now we no longer have to tolerate being mistreated. We now have a choice.

Integration often comes at between three and five years of a full recovery program. When stress comes up that knocks us back to a survival-stage feeling again, we are now able to awaken and recognize a core issue rapidly, cycle through the transformation stage rapidly, reminding ourself of what is happening and how not to be mistreated and that we do have boundaries and choices (Gravitz, Bowden, 1986). We no longer have to waste our energy on denial, because we now sense and see things for what they really are. Relative to our past, we are stuck for only a very short time.

We no longer have to stop to think consciously about what is happening — although it is okay to do so. Now we just do it. We fully reclaim our Real Self, including *being* real when we feel like it, and deciding when *not* to be real in certain situations or around certain people. When we do experience a loss, feel frightened, upset or age-regress, we re-cycle it, sometimes quickly, sometimes slowly.

We establish appropriate boundaries and limits with people. If people continue to run roughshod over us or ignore us, we say either, "No, you can't do that anymore" or we get out. We don't stand in the rain anymore and pretend it isn't raining (Gravitz, Bowden, 1986). We are no longer victims or martyrs.

Our journey thus far in healing our Child Within can be summarized, in part, in the following poem by Portia Nelson.

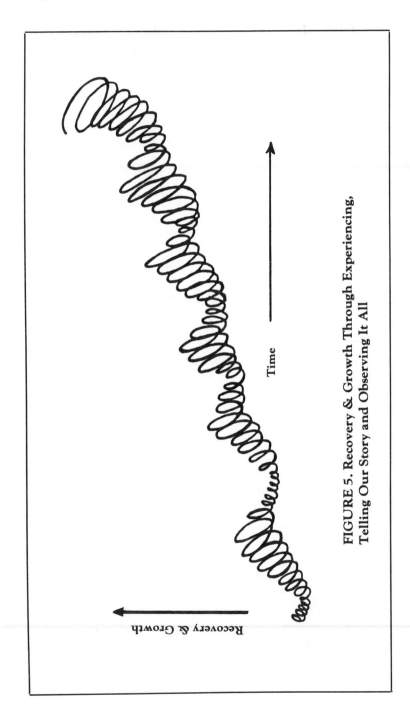

FIGURE 5. Recovery & Growth Through Experiencing, Telling Our Story and Observing It All

Autobiography in Five Short Chapters

1) I walk, down the street.
 There is a deep hole in the sidewalk.
 I fall in.
 I am lost . . . I am hopeless.
  It isn't my fault.
 It takes forever to find a way out.

2) I walk down the same street.
 There is a deep hole in the sidewalk.
 I pretend I don't see it.
 I fall in again.
 I can't believe I am in the same place.
  But, it isn't my fault.
 It still takes a long time to get out.

3) I walk down the same street.
 There is a deep hole in the sidewalk.
 I see it is there.
 I still fall in . . . it's a habit.
  My eyes are open
  I know where I am.
 It is **my** fault.
 I get out immediately.

4) I walk down the same street.
 There is a deep hole in the sidewalk.
 I walk around it.

5) I walk down another street.

Chapter 15

The Role of Spirituality

Spirituality is so vast an area in recovery that in this brief chapter I can only begin to describe it. Yet it is very helpful — some say crucial — in healing our Child Within.

Spirituality is the last "stage" in our recovery. And paradoxically, it can never be a stage, since it is an ongoing process throughout suffering, healing and serenity.

Beginning to Define Spirituality

In perhaps one of its briefest definitions spirituality is about the *relationships* that we have with our self, with others and with the universe. It is characterized by several key concepts and principles, one of which is that it is *paradoxical*. Otherwise seemingly opposite conditions, entities or experiences coexist comfortably together. For example, spirituality is both *subtle* and *powerful*. It is like our breath. We go about most of our day not even realizing that we are breathing. Yet our breathing is so powerful that if we stop, we die.

Spirituality is *personal*. Each of us has to discover it on our own, in our own way. It is highly *useful*, in that it deals with a spectrum of life issues, from learning basic trust to getting free of suffering. And spirituality is *experiential*. To appreciate it, we use it, to realize it, we have to experience it. We cannot know it ultimately through our intellect or through reason. It is not knowable. It is only be-able.

It is *indescribable*. It is so vast, that even if we were to read all of the world's great holy books and listen to all of the great spiritual masters, we would still not fathom it. Spirituality is *inclusive* and *supportive*. It does not reject any thing. And here is where organized religion may enter, because it is a part of spirituality. Thus, while *spirituality is not organized religion*, it includes it, supports it and then transcends it.

It is *healing* and *growth-inducing*, and thus is ultimately *fulfilling*. The journey of discovery and healing described throughout this book is actually and ultimately a spiritual journey, although we usually do not view it as such at its beginning. As we enter and work through each healing stage, we move to the next stage. And when we move from one stage to the next, we do not abandon or cancel the former stages. Rather, we *transcend* them, which means that while we still respect and use them as is appropriate and spontaneous for us, we are now operating and living our life from an entirely new level of consciousness, awareness and being. These levels of consciousness parallel several descriptions of our spiritual path.

Viewing Our "Spiritual Path"

In the 1940s and 1950s Maslow described a hierarchy of human needs (see Table 14). These progress from bottom to top, as: (1) Physiological, basic functioning or survival; (2) Safety; (3) the sense of Belonging and Love; (4) Self-actualization, *i.e.*, knowing and being comfortable with our True Self; and (5) Transcendence or spirituality, *i.e.*, fully realizing our True Self, our Higher Self. These parallel the needs described in Chapter 4 and Table 2, where our human needs are listed in more detail. They also parallel the discovery and recovery of our Child Within described throughout this book. And finally, they parallel our levels of human awareness or consciousness.

As we learn various ways of looking at, conceptualizing and "mapping" our journey of recovery, we see that these are similar, perhaps even the same journey looked at in a slightly different way. These three ways also parallel the path of the 12-Steps of recovery: surviving active alcoholism (or chemical dependence, co-dependence, overeating, or other mistreatment and suffering), then admission of a problem, and then changing our isolation to

TABLE 14. Similar Hierarchies of Human Needs, Development and Consciousness

Maslow's Needs	Healing Child Within	Level of Consciousness
		Unity
	Using Spirituality	
		Compassion
Transcendence		
	Integrating	Understanding (creativity, natural knowing)
Self-actualization	Transforming	Acceptance thru Conflict (Heart)
	Dealing with core issues (Exploring)	"Power" (mind, ego, "identity")
Belonging and love	Awakening (emergent awareness)	
Safety		Passion (emotions, basic sexuality)
Physiological	Surviving	Survival (food, shelter, illness)

sharing, including eventually with a Higher Power. As we progress in working the Steps, next comes self-examination, catharsis and personality change, followed by improved relationships, helping others and then discovering serenity.

As we grow in healing our Child Within, we begin to notice that our child is not limited to only one or two levels of being, awareness or consciousness. Rather, our Child Within also parallels and exists along these same seven levels, as shown in Table 15.

Helpless Infant

Reading from bottom to top of Table 15, we note that a part of our Child is a Helpless Infant. It wants and needs to be cared for and nurtured. As we cycle through our developmental stages, we first need affection, caring and nurturing. Only when we have had these needs met are we ready to move to the next stage of our development. Since many neglected or mistreated children did not get their needs met in this way, they did not complete their development at this level. Part of the task of recovery is learning to get our needs met and get nurtured so that we can begin to re-cycle through this stage and thus complete our unfinished development in it.

We also discover that there is only one person that can assure that we get the nurturing that we need, and that one person is *us.* But it is not we as our co-dependent self. Rather, it is we as our Total Child Within. Our Child Within is thus both our nurturer *and* that Helpless Infant that needs so desperately to be nurtured, and it is all the other parts. *We are our own nurturer.* We have to assure that we get what we need. We may at times get others to help us get what we need, but basically we are the only one that can attend to our needs. I describe our needs in Table 2 of Chapter 4.

TABLE 15. Levels of Being, Awareness or Consciousness of Our Child Within

---

- Unconditionally loving Child
- Compassionate Child
- Creative Child
- Struggling and growing Child
- Thinking and reasoning Child
- Feeling Child
- Helpless Infant

Feeling Child

The Feeling Child within us is full of feelings and emotions. Like all seven levels of being of our Child Within, it is interconnected with each of the other levels. Our Feeling Child lets us know when we need to attend to something. That something might be something wrong, like a real danger or a hurt, or something pleasant, or it might be a feeling reaction from the past that comes up. Whatever it is, we are now attentive to it (see Chapter 10 on Feelings).

Thinking and Reasoning Child

Our Thinking and Reasoning Child is related to our ego, mind or self. It is that which many people think they are — their "identity." It is also often mistaken for the seat of "power." Yet it is only one part of us.

Our Thinking and Reasoning Child is perhaps the part of our True Self that is the most directly connected to our co-dependent self. We might even say that they are friends. More than any other, it understands our co-dependent self and so will be able to work with it when we *need* our co-dependent self. Many people have an exaggeration or overdevelopment of their Thinking and Reasoning Child and their co-dependent self.

As we recover we bring into play the other parts of our Child Within, and we become more balanced, integrated, individuated and whole.

Struggling and Growing Child

Our Struggling and Growing Child is the equivalent of the "Heart" level of consciousness and is the key to our Higher Self and to realizing serenity. It is the link between our Higher Self and our lower self. It is perhaps best described by the phrase "acceptance through conflict." This means coming to accept "what is" by first recognizing or becoming aware of it, then working through the pain *or* enjoying the pleasure, and then coming to peace with it. It is analogous to the grieving process, the process of forgiveness — turning it over — detachment — letting go, and to the process of telling our story, in that it *uses* these processes to accept and to grow.

Creative Child

Have you ever sensed or *known* that something was true or right, and you didn't need any rational explanation to prove it? Our Creative Child is one that uses what men call "hunches" or "gut reactions" and what women call "intuition" to assist them in their lives. This is the part of us that knows naturally and inherently. Ideas, inspirations and creative sparks come up to us through this part of our Child regularly, throughout our lives. For example, this part of us is where we might say most of the great works of art, science, literature and play originate.

However, our co-dependent self may at times try to disguise itself as our Creative Child and its "intuitions" will often mislead us. Thus we can check out any inspirations or intuitions that come to us and see how they turn out. If they work for us, they are likely to originate in our Creative Child. If they do not, they may have come from our false self. There are several books available on this topic such as Frances Vaughan's *Awakening Intuition* and my *Alcoholism and Spirituality.*

Compassionate Child

Have you ever been with someone and on listening to their story you became so touched or moved that a tear came to your eyes? Yet at the same time while you knew they were suffering or had suffered and/or experienced joy, you knew that it would *not* be helpful to try to rescue them or try to change them? When we have such an experience, we are in direct contact with our Compassionate Child. In fact, at this instant we *are* our Compassionate Child.

Our Compassionate Child is a sort of mirror image or direct opposite of our Passionate Child. Our Passionate Child may want to try to fix, rescue or change the other person. We may also notice that our Creative Child is the mirror image of our Thinking and Reasoning Child, and that our Unconditionally Loving Child is the mirror image of our Helpless Infant (Table 15).

Unconditionally Loving Child

This part of us is for many the most difficult to comprehend and to be. We were perhaps so mistreated growing up — and for some of us are still being mistreated — that we are unable to love anyone unconditionally, including ourselves. Because of this difficulty, and because I believe that this is a core recovery issue for adult children of trauma, I will discuss it in more detail.

Love and Unconditional Love

Low self-esteem, a sense of inherent defectiveness and unworthiness, is a common experience among those of us who have been mistreated. It is also common among those who have developed an illness such as alcoholism, chemical dependence, co-dependence, an eating disorder or a similar condition wherein one feels like a victim. Related to several important factors, including inability to control alcohol, drugs, eating, other people *or whatever,* we believe that we are simply not worthy of receiving love.

Rather than believe we are unlovable, we can shift to believing that we do not *need* love. This translates into, "I don't want to be loved," and then finally to "I will reject love, no matter who gives it to me" (Gravitz, Bowden, 1985). We end up with "frozen feelings" or an inability to fully experience feelings and emotions especially including love.

It is often in recovery where we experience the unconditional love of a self-help group, a therapy group, a counselor, sponsor or a trusted friend, that we begin to feel the healing effects of love. Indeed love is the most healing of our resources, and it takes several years of being so loved to get well and stay well. And then we can begin to love others in return.

A problem for many of us is that we often view love as a limited experience or entity, such as that of "falling in love" or infatuation. In our recovery we learn that love is not simply a feeling. Rather it is an *energy* that is manifested by a *commitment and a will to extend oneself for the purpose of nurturing one's own or another's total growth,* which includes physical, mental, emotional and spiritual dimensions (Peck, 1978).

As we grow in recovery we begin to see that there are several different kinds of love. I outline these in Table 16 according to our seven levels of consciousness. By such a view, we see that in the lower self, love is neediness, "chemistry" or infatuation, possession, strong admiration or even worship — in short, traditional romantic love. Many people who grew up in troubled homes and who experienced a stifling of their Child Within become stuck at these lower levels or ways of experiencing love. In healing our Child Within we eventually discover, work through and transcend to higher levels of love including caring through conflict, forgiveness, trust, commitment to growth in ourself and in a loved one, unconditional empathy and acceptance, and pure peaceful

Being. By recognizing, experiencing and letting go, and by using the spiritual practices described and taught by many, we can gradually open to the Love within each of us (Whitfield, 1985).

Finally we learn that love is what we and what our Higher Power, as we understand it, use to heal ourselves. It is what is ultimately healing in group therapy, counseling, friendships, meditation, prayer or whatever. *We no longer have to be afraid of love or to run away from it, because we know that it is inside us as the core and healing part of our Child Within.*

Our Observer Self

As we evolve and grow in our recovery we discover that there is a part of us, perhaps located somewhere in the Higher Self of our Child Within, that is able to step back and to watch, witness or observe what is happening in our life. For example, many people have experienced becoming extremely upset and then detaching from their upset and feelings to such an extent that they find themselves actually observing themselves in the upset. Sometimes there is an out-of-body experience, so that they are able to see themselves or a representation of themselves having the upset. This ability can be facilitated by practicing guided or eidedic imagery and visualizations (Small, 1985). Closing the eyes, the person visualizes or otherwise imagines the scene or activity about which there is concern. One can then visualize a positive solution to the upset. This can also be done while meditating. Done constructively, this is a healthy practice.

Deikman (1982) and others call this powerful and freeing part of us the observer or observing self. The Western psychological literature refers to the observing self as "the observing ego" but does not explore the special nature of the "ego" and its implications for understanding of the self. It thus continues to miss the dynamics, meaning and importance of the observer self, and its theories of the self remain somewhat confused.

The observing self is central to our recovery. An illustration is shown in Figure 6. This shows the interrelationships of the self (or "object self") and the observing self. The self is concerned with thinking, feeling, acting, desiring and other survival-oriented activities. (This older and less useful concept of the self includes parts of both the false self and the True Self.) However, the observer self, a part of who we really are, is that part of us that is

TABLE 16. Defining Some Clinical Therapeutic Properties of the Self (Levels 4 through 7): Love, Truth, Healing & Power along the Levels of Human Consciousness. (Levels 1 through 3 re-present those for the lower self) (From Whitfield, 1985)

Hierarchy of Consciousness	Love	Truth	Healing	Power
7) Unity consciousness	Peaceful being	Peaceful being	Peaceful being	Peaceful being
6) Compassion	Unconditional empathy and acceptance	Love and acceptance	Love and acceptance	Love and acceptance
5) Understanding	Commitment to growth	Creativity	Right decision	Wisdom
4) Acceptance/heart	Forgiveness	Forgiveness	Forgiveness	Forgiveness
3) Mind/ego	Worship Possession	Experience Beliefs	Prevention, education Psychologic	Assertion Persuasion
2) Passion	"Chemistry"	Sensations	Nurturance	Manipulation
1) Survival	Neediness	Science	Physical	Physical strength

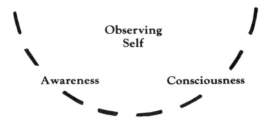

Aspects of the self

Thinking, Planning, Solving, Worrying
Emotion, Feeling, Affect
Action, Behavior, Functioning
Desire, Wish, Fantasy

FIGURE 6. Relationship of the Observing Self and
the self (object self) (compiled from Deikman, 1982)

watching both our false self and our True Self. We might say that
it even watches us when we watch. It *is* our Consciousness, it is
the core experience of our Child Within. It thus cannot be
watched — at least by any thing or any being that we know of on
this earth. It transcends our five senses, our co-dependent self and
all other lower, though necessary, parts of us.

Adult children may confuse their observer self with a kind of
defense they may have used to avoid their Real Self and all of its
feelings. One might call this defense a "false observer self" since
its awareness is clouded. It is unfocused as it "spaces" or "numbs-
out." It denies and distorts our Child Within, and is often judgmental. By contrast, our True Observer Self has a clearer awareness, observes more accurately, and tends to be accepting. The
following outlines these differences.

**Some Differences Between the True Observer Self and The
False Observer Self**

	True	False
Awareness	Clearer	Clouded
Focus	Observes	"Spaces Out" or "Numbs Out"
Feelings	Observes Accurately	Denies
Attitude	Accepting	Judgmental

Expanding our consciousness, we can soon become aware of our part in the larger drama — the "cosmic drama." By watching our own personal dance or melodrama, we can begin to learn that our Observer Self is that part of us which, when we realize we are "really carrying on," can step back and observe the carrying on, through the power of our imagination. By doing so, we often bring into play the powerful defense of humor, e.g., by laughing at ourself for taking it all so seriously.

Deikman (1982) said, "The observing self is not part of the object world formed by our thoughts and sensory perception because, literally, it has no limits; everything else does. Thus everyday consciousness contains a transcendent element that we seldom notice because that element is the very ground of our experience. The word transcendent is justified because if subjective consciousness — the observing self — cannot itself be observed but remains forever apart from the contents of consciousness, it is likely to be a different order from everything else. Its fundamentally different nature becomes evident when we realize that the observing self is featureless; it cannot be affected by the world any more than a mirror can be affected by the images it reflects."

As our observer self becomes more prominent, our lower or object self tends to recede. Primary identification with our lower self tends to be associated with suffering and illness. However, building a strong and flexible ego or object self which is part of healing our Child Within, is usually required before we can transition into our observer self for any lasting duration.

Realizing Serenity

As we become more familiar with being our observer self and with the healing power of spirituality, we can begin to construct a possible path to realizing serenity, inner peace and happiness. I have condensed the following description from *Alcoholism and Spirituality,* where each is discussed in more detail.

Some Possible Paths to Serenity

1. We are ignorant of our Journey, we are limited (humility): we can study universal "laws," approximate them and surrender to our lack of ultimate knowledge. Given these limitations, sages over the centuries describe something like the following:

2. Higher Power is in each of us, and we are in Higher Power.

3. We can view our reality as a hierarchy of levels of awareness, consciousness or being.

4. We are going Home (we *are* Home, already and always). Home on this earth is being all levels of our awareness or consciousness in our own unique fashion.

5. There will be conflict going Home (melodrama, cosmic drama). This conflict or creative tension is useful to us in some way, probably as a way Home.

6. We have a choice. We can use our bodies, ego/minds, our relationships on this earth to reinforce our separation and our suffering. Or we can use them as vehicles for our Soul, Spirit or Higher Self to return Home and to celebrate that return.

7. Higher Power (Home) is Love (Love is perhaps the most useful way we know Higher Power).

8. We can remove the blocks to realizing our Higher Power by experiencing (including living in the Now), remembering, forgiving and surrendering (these five realizations can be viewed as being ultimately the same). Regular spiritual practices help us with this realization.

9. Separation, suffering and evil are the absence of realizing Love, and are therefore ultimately illusions. They are also manifestations of our searching for Love, Wholeness, and Home. The evil or darkness is thus ultimately in the service of the light.

10. We create our own story by our thoughts and actions. What we think and feel in our mind and heart, we will produce in our experience and our life. What we give, we get. As within, so without.

11. Life is a Process, Force or Flow that lives us. We do not live it. When we surrender to it, *i.e.*, flow with its Process and take responsibility for our participation in it, we become co-creators. We can then become free of our suffering that comes with our attachment to resisting flowing with our Life.

12. Inner peace or serenity is knowing, practicing and being all of the above. We ultimately discover that we are already and always Serenity and Home.

Some sources: Perennial Philosophy (Huxley), Christ, Tao, Mukta-nanda, A Course in Miracles, Fox, Wilber, Lazaris, Schuan, and many other thinkers and sages.

Some of these principles are illustrated in the following case history of James, a 42-year-old man who grew up in an alcoholic family, his father being the actively drinking alcoholic and his mother usually assuming the role of a placating co-dependent. While he showed no manifestations of being alcoholic himself throughout his adult life, James was progressively aware of his inordinate confusion and suffering. He eventually attended Al-Anon and later, ACoA self-help group meetings, for a total of about six years, with some improvement. He describes the importance and meaning of the spiritual part of his recovery as follows.

"I went to a lot of Al-Anon and then ACoA self-help meetings over these years, probably one or two a week. I really wanted to get well. But I didn't seem to be doing it, although something seemed to keep me motivated to keep attending. I had always thought it was important for me to be strong, which I equated with being independent. This meant to me not to talk much. I believed I could recover on my own, without anyone's help. I equated weakness with trusting, surrendering or being dependent, all of which I saw as being a kind of sickness. I viewed people with these char-acteristics as being sick. And, of course, I felt I was healthier or somehow better than they were. Looking back I see all of this as a probably necessary defense that allowed me to keep attending the meetings without being too overwhelmed by my hidden feelings and the changes I needed to make to recover.

"During that time I met a woman at the meetings who was really arrogant and unhappy. She was so obnoxious to me that I tried to avoid being around the meetings she attended.

I thought there was no hope for her and that I was certainly better than she was. Then I saw her change. She started to lose her arrogant attitude and became friendlier to me and to others. She seemed happy. While I hated to admit it since it was coming from her who I had never admired, I felt envious of her positive change. I wanted some of that. But she was also *now* talking about her Higher Power, and I have always had trouble knowing what that was, even though I had had a fairly active religious upbringing.

"So I began considering what had happened to her and how I might get some of that peace or happiness. It began to occupy a lot of my thoughts and feelings. I'd been through 40 years of unhappiness and confusion. I began to read some spiritual literature, and I began to pray. While I had tried to pray since I was a child, there was something different about my praying this time. Perhaps I was more sincere and humble. Then some months later I experienced a kind of transformation that came on me over about a two-week period. My own attitude changed and I let go of my resentments of my father and of others. (Of course, I had done a lot of work in the past on my anger and other feelings, as well as other issues of mine.) I began to really believe in a Higher Power, something I'd never been able to do. I had first reframed health as happiness and then reframed happiness as being associated with needing others and surrendering to them and to a spiritual program. Doing so has made all the difference."

James' story illustrates several of the principles of ways to realize serenity (see above list). First, he experienced conflict and struggle (#5 above). He used this struggle in his uncomfortable relationship with the woman he resented as a vehicle for his spiritual evolution and growth (#6). He was aware of his conflict and pain, and he began a regular spiritual practice — prayer (#8). He eventually asked for what he wanted, this time with sincerity and humility (#10), and he surrendered to the Process of his life (#11). Ultimately, he found what he was seeking, and it was inside himself and nowhere else (#12).

The traditional or conventional views of attaining serenity, inner peace or happiness usually uses one or both of either seeking pleasure or avoiding pain. In the *seeking* approach, the ways of seeking happiness may span a range from hedonistic seeking to focusing on others (which can result in co-dependence) to "being good" and waiting to claim our peace later as a reward in Heaven. In the *avoiding pain* approach we may try to ignore pain, detach from it or stay away from any situation that might bring on conflict for us. We may ask, "Has either seeking or avoiding ever brought us lasting peace, happiness or serenity?" When I have asked this of others and of myself, the answer is usually "no."

In response one of our choices is to feel hurt and resentful about our inability to be happy, and to project our pain onto others. Or as a second alternative, we might begin to *observe* the whole process and begin to observe the "self-contraction" of our co-dependent self, when we are unhappy. As we do so we can begin to see that happiness is not something that we *attain*. Rather happiness, peace or serenity is our *natural state*. Beneath all of what we *add* to our feelings and experience, beneath our self-contraction, lies Serenity Itself. To realize serenity there is nothing that we need to do or even that we can do. If we make all As on our report card, that won't do it. Neither will owning three Rolls Royces, nor will having a million dollars or marrying a "Ms. or Mr. Right." There is no way that we can earn or achieve happiness, and neither is there any way that we can deserve it. Rather, it is ours *inherently*, already and always (Da Free John, 1985).

For adult children of trauma accepting this idea that we are inherently happy may be difficult. If that is so, I think I can understand. As we heal our Child Within this realization that we are already and always happy becomes easier and easier. I have found that doing a daily spiritual practice, such as meditation or prayer, and reading spiritual literature has been helpful in realizing my own serenity.

Some readers may be skeptical about this concept of "spirituality." Some may be confused. Others may not believe any of it and may even feel like "this author sure has lost it now!" By contrast others may find some solace in reading it, and still others may identify a lot of useful material here. Whatever your reaction, I invite you to follow your reactions and instincts. Reflect upon it, talk about it whenever you may sense that it is appropriate. Use what you can, and leave the rest. Spirituality has worked for me and I have seen it work for hundreds of others in healing their Child Within.

Appendix:
A Note On
Recovery Methods

Many clinicians who work with adult children of alcoholics or other troubled or dysfunctional families believe that *group therapy* is the major *treatment of choice* for recovery work. I believe this to be true when it is integrated with a *full recovery program* of:

- Treatment of any active addiction, compulsion or attachment (e.g., active alcoholism/CD, an eating disorder, etc.)
- Self-help group attendance, using a sponsor and working the 12 steps or similar concepts of recovery,
- Education about the condition and about recovery techniques,
- Inpatient treatment — brief and intensive; as desired or recommended,
- Individual counseling or psychotherapy as indicated.

I believe that consideration of all these are part of a wholistic physical, mental, emotional and spiritual recovery program that is ongoing. Given these reservations, the following are *some advantages* of the major *treatment of choice* — group therapy.

Some Advantages of Group Therapy for Adult Children

1) The group member has several "therapists," instead of just one (I recommend having two group leaders and between seven and ten members in each group, depending on the regularity of attendance).
2) The group re-creates many aspects of their family and thereby provides them a vehicle to work through the emotional ties, conflicts, and struggles (transference, *i.e.*, projection) associated with their own family.
3) The person gets to see recovery modeled in several stages. Especially motivating and healing is the ability to see people come into group and make definitive and at times dramatic positive changes in their lives and in healing their own Child Within.

4) With appropriately trained and skilled group leaders, the group is able to work on specific life issues that span the range of physical, mental, emotional and spiritual recovery.
5) The well-known advantages of group therapy in general, such as the ability to obtain identification, validation, feedback, appropriate confrontation, support and the many other useful factors and dynamics in group therapy.

Developing enough skills and momentum of self-healing to overcome and replace the negative conditioning, victim stance and repetition compulsion and to discover and heal our Child Within usually takes from three to five years of working such a full recovery program.

Recovery is not an intellectual or rational process. Nor is it easy. It is an experiential process, consisting of excitement, discouragement, pain and joy, with an overall pattern of personal growth. Recovery takes great courage. Even though it cannot be explained adequately with words alone, I have begun to describe this process of healing the Child Within.

References

Ackerman, R.J.: Children of Alcoholics: A Guidebook for Educators, Therapists and Parents (2nd ed.). Learning Publications, Holmes Beach, Florida, 1983.

Ackerman, R.J.: Growing in the Shadow. Health Communications, Pompano Beach, Florida, 1986.

Adult Children of Alcoholics (ACA — Central Service Board) Box 3216, Los Angeles, California 90505.

Al-Anon Family Groups, P.O. Box 182, Madison Square Station, New York 10159.

American Psychiatric Association DSM-III: Diagnostic and Statistical Manual of Mental Disorders (3rd ed.). Washington, DC, 1980.

Armstrong T.: The Radiant Child. Quest, Wheaton, Illinois, 1985.

Beattie, M.: Codependent No More. Hazelden, Center City, Minnesota, 1987.

Black, C.: It Will Never Happen To Me. Medical Administration Colorado, 1980.

Black, C.: Talk on Adult Children of Alcoholics, Gambrills, Maryland, 1984.

Booz, Allan & Hamilton, Inc.: An Assessment of the Needs and Resources for the Children of Alcoholic Parents. NIAAA Contract Report, 1974.

Bowlby, J.: Loss. Basic Books, New York, 1980.

Bowlby, J.: On knowing what you are not supposed to know and feeling what you are not supposed to feel. J. Canadian Psychiatric Assoc., 1979.

Bowden, J.D. & Gravitz, H.L.: Genesis. Health Communications, Pompano Beach, FL, 1987.

Briggs, D.C.: Your Child's Self-Esteem: Step-by-step Guidelines to Raising Responsible, Productive, Happy Children. Doubleday Dolphin Books, Garden City, New York 1970.

Briggs, D.C.: Embracing Life: Growing Through Love and Loss. Doubleday, Garden City, New York, 1985.

Brooks, C.: The Secret Everyone Knows. Kroc Foundation, San Diego, California, 1981.

Brown, S.: Presentation at Second National Conference on Children of Alcoholics, Washington, DC, 26 February, 1986.

Campbell, J.: The Hero With a Thousand Faces. Princeton Univ. Press, 1949.

Cermak, T.L.: A Primer for Adult Children of Alcoholics. Health Communications, Pompano Beach, Florida, 1985.

Cermak, T.L., Brown, S.: Interactional group therapy with the adult children of alcoholics. *International Journal Group Psychotherapy.* 32:375-389, 1982.

Cermak, T.L.: Diagnosing & Treating Co-Dependence: A Guide for Professionals who Work with Chemical Dependents, Their Spouses, and Children. Johnson Institute, Minneapolis, Minnesota, 1986.

Clarke, J.I.: Self-Esteem: A Family Affair. Harper/Winston, Minneapolis, Minnesota, 1978.

Colgrave, M., Bloomfield, H., McWilliams: How to Survive the Loss of a Love. Bantam Books, New York, 1976.

Cork, M.: The Forgotten Children. Addiction Research Foundation, Toronto, Canada, 1969.

A Course in Miracles. Foundation for Inner Peace, Tiburon, California, 1976.

Deikman, A.J.: The Observing Self. Beacon Press, Boston, Massachusetts, 1982.

Deutsch, C.: Broken Bottles, Broken Dreams: Understanding and Helping the Children of Alcoholics. Teachers College Press, New York, 1982.

Dossey, L: Beyond Illness: Discovering the Experience of Health. Shambhala, Boulder, Colorado, 1985.

Dreitlein, R.: Feelings in Recovery. Workshop, Rutgers Summer School on Alcohol Studies, New Brunswick, New Jersey, 1984.

Eisenberg, L.: Normal child development. In Freedman, A.M.; Kaplan, H.I. (eds.): The Child: His Psychological and Cultural Development. Vol. 2, The major psychological disorders and their development. Atheneum, New York, 1972.

Epstein, G.: The Image in Medicine: Notes of a Clinician. *Advances.* Vol. 3, Winter, 1986.

Faukhauser, J.: From a Chicken to an Eagle: What Happens When You Change. Coleman Graphics, Farmingdale, New York, 1984.

Ferguson, M.: The Aquarian Conspiracy: Personal and Social Transformation in the 1980's. Tarcher, Los Angeles, California, 1980.

Finn, C.C.: Poem previously unpublished by author, and published several times attributed to "Anonymous" by others. Written in Chicago,

1966. Here published by permission of the author, personal communication, Fincastle, Virginia, March, 1986.

Fischer, B.: Workshop on Shame. The Resource Group, Baltimore, Maryland, 1985.

Forward, S.; Buck, C.: Betrayal of Innocence: Incest and its Devastation. Penguin Books, New York, 1978.

Fossum, M.A.; Mason, M.J.: Facing Shame: Families in Recovery. WW Norton, New York, 1986.

Fox, E.: Reawakening the Power of Your Wonder Child. In Power Through Constructive Thinking. Harper & Row, New York, 1940.

Freud, A.: The Ego and the Mechanisms of Defense. Revised Ed. Int'l Unversities Press, New York, 1966.

Gil, E.: Outgrowing the Pain. A Book for and about Adults Abused as Children. Launch Press, Box 40174, San Francisco, California 94140, 1984.

George, D.; Richo, D.: Workshop on Child Within. Santa Barbara, California, April, 1986.

Gravitz, H.L.; Bowden, J.D.: Guide to Recovery: A Book for Adult Children of Alcoholics. Learning Publications, Holmes Beach, Florida, 1985.

Grossman, W.I.: The Self as Fantasy: Fantasy as Theory. *J. American Psychoanalytical Assoc.*, 30: 919-937, 1982.

Guntrip, H.: Psychoanalytical Theory, Therapy and the Self: A Basic Guide to the Human Personality, in Freud, Erickson, Klein, Sullivan, Fairbairn, Hartman, Jacobsen and Winnicott. Basic Books, Harper Torchbooks, New York, 1973.

Hayward, J.; Thomas, R.: Watching and Waiting. Song by Moody Blues, Threshold Records.

Helmstetter, S.: What to Say When You Talk to Yourself. Grindle Press, Scottsdale, Arizona, 1986.

Hillman, J.: Healing Fiction. Station Hill, Barrytown, New York, 1983.

Hillman, J.: Abandoning the Child. In Loose Ends: Primary Papers in Archtypal Psychology. Spring Publications, Dallas, Texas, 1975.

Hoffman, B.: No One Is To Blame: Getting a Loving Divorce From Mom and Dad. Science and Behavior Books, Palo Alto, California, 1979.

Horney, K.: Chap. 71. The Holistic Approach (Horney). By Kelman, H. in American Handbook of Psychiatry. Basic Books, NY, 1959.

Jackson, M.: Self-Like Seminar. Los Angeles, California, 1986.

James, M.; Savary, L.: A New Self: Self Therapy with Transactional Analysis. Addison-Wesley, Reading, Massachusetts, 1977.

Jacoby, M.: the Analytical Encounter: Transference and Human Relationship. Inner City Books, Toronto, Canada, 1984.

Jourard, S.M.: The Transparent Self. Van Nostrand, New York, 1971.

Jung, C.G.: Kerenyi, C.: Essays on a Science of Mythology: The Myth of the Divine Child. Billingen Series, Princeton, 1969.

Kagan, J.: The Nature of the Child. Basic Books, New York, 1984.

Kanner, L.: History of Child Psychiatry. In Freedman, A.M. and Kaplan, H.I. (eds.): The Child: His Psychological and Cultural Development. Vol. 2. The Major Psychological Disorders and Their Development. Athaeneum, New York, 1972.

Kaufman, G.: Shame: The Power of Caring. Schenkman, Cambridge, Massachusetts, 1980.

Kohut, H.: The Analysis of the Self. International Univ. Press, New York, 1971.

Kritsberg, W.: The Adult Children of Alcoholics Syndrome: From Discovery to Recovery. Health Communications, Pompano Beach, Florida, 1986.

Kurtz, E.: Not-God: A History of Alcoholism Anonymous. Hazelden Educational Services, Center City, Minnesota, 1979.

Kurtz, E.: Shame and Guilt: Characteristics of the Dependency Cycle (an Historical Perspective for Professionals). Hazelden, Center City, Minnesota, 1981.

Lazaris: Series of Spiritual-Psychological Teachings. Available from Concept Synergy, 302 S. County Rd., Palm Beach, Florida 33408.

Levin, P.: Cycles of Power: A Guidebook for the Seven Stages of Life. Dissertation, 1980. Available from Trans Publications, 1259 El Camino Real, Menlo Park, California 94025.

Lindemann, E.: The Symptomatology and Management of Acute Grief. *Amer. J. of Psychiatry,* 101: 141-148, 1944.

Masterson, J.F.: The Real Self: A Developmental, Self and Objective Relations Approach. Brunner/Mazel, New York, 1985.

Matthews-Simonton, S., in Simonton, Matthews-Simonton Creighton: Getting Well Again. Bantam Books, New York, 1978.

Middelton-Moz, J.; Dwinell, L.: After the Tears: Reclaiming the Personal Losses of Childhood. Health Communications, Pompano Beach, Florida, 1986.

Miller, A.: The Drama of the Gifted Child. Harper, New York, 1981 and 1983.

Miller, A.: For Your Own Good: Hidden Cruelty in Childrearing and the Roots of Violence. Farrar, Strauss, Giroux, New York, 1983.

Miller, A.: Pictures of a Childhood. Farrar, Strauss, Giroux, New York, 1986.

Miller, A.: Thou Shall Not Be Aware: Society's Betrayal of the Child. Farrar, Straus, Giroux, New York, 1984.

Missildine, W.H.: Your Inner Child of the Past. Pocket Books, New York, 1963.

Moss, R.: How Shall I Live: Transforming Surgery or Any Health Crisis Into Greater Aliveness. Celestial Arts, Berkeley, California, 1985.

National Association for Children of Alcoholics. 31706 Coast Highway, Suite 201, South Laguna, California 92677, (Tel. 714-499-3889).

Nelson, P.: Autobiography in Five Short Chapters. In Nelson P.: There's a Hole in My Sidewalk. Popular Library, New York, 1977.

Pearce, J.C.: Magical Child: Rediscovering Nature's Plan for Our Children. Bantam Books, New York, 1986.

Peck, M.S.: The Road Less Traveled: A New Psychology of Love, Traditional Values, and Spiritual Growth. Simon & Schuster, New York, 1978.

Rose, A.L., et al.: The Feel Wheel. Center for Studies of the Person. LaJolla, California, 1972.

Samuel, W.: "The Child Within Us Lives!" Mountain Brook Pub., Mountain Brook, Alabama, 1986.

Satir, V.: Peoplemaking. Science & Behavior Books, Palo Alto, California, 1972.

Schaef, A.W.: Co-dependence: Misdiagnosed and Mistreated. Harper/Winston, Minneapolis, 1986.

Schatzman, M.: Soul Murder: Persecution in the Family. New York, 1973.

Siegel, B.S.: Love, Medicine and Miracles: Lessons Learned About Self-Healing from a Surgeon's Experience with Exceptional Patients. Harper & Row, New York, 1986.

Siegel, B.S.; Siegel, B.: Spiritual Aspects of the Healing Arts. In Kunz, D. (ed.): Spiritual Aspects of the Healing Arts, Quest, Wheaton, Illinois, 1985.

Seixas, J.S.; Youcha, G.: Children of Alcoholism: A Survivor's Manual. Crown, New York, 1985.

Simos, B.G.: A Time to Grieve: Loss as a Universal Human Experience. Family Services Association of America, New York, 1979.

Small, J.: Transformers: Therapists of the Future. DeVorrs, Los Angeles, California, 1986.

Spitz, R.: Hospitalism in the Psychoanalytic Study of the Child. Vol. 1, Int'l. Univ. Press, New York, 1945.

Steere, D.V: GLEANINGS, Upper Room, Nashville, Tennessee, 1986.

Vaughan, F.: Awakening Intuition. Anchor/Doubleday, New York, 1979.

Vaughan, F.: The Inward Arc: Healing & Wholeness in Psychotherapy and Spirituality. Shambhala, Boston, Massachusetts, 1985.

Viorst, J.: Necessary Losses: The Loves, Illusions, Dependencies and Impossible Expectations That All of Us Have to Give Up in Order to Grow. Simon & Schuster, New York, 1986.

Viscott, D.: The Language of Feelings. Pocket Books, New York, 1976.

Ward, M.: The Brilliant Function of Pain. Optimus Books, New York, 1977.

Wegscheider, S.: Another Chance: Hope and Health for the Alcoholic Family. Science and Behavior Books, Palo Alto, California, 1981.

Wegscheider-Cruse, S.: Choice-Making: For Co-Dependents, Adult Children and Spirituality Seekers. Health Communications, Pompano Beach, Florida, 1985.

Weil, A.: The Natural Mind. Houghton Mifflin, New York, 1972.

Wheelis, A.: How People Change. Harper/Colophon, New York, 1983.

Whitfield, C.L.: Alcoholism and Medical Education. *Maryland State Med. J.*, October, 1980.

Whitfield, C.L.: Children of Alcoholics; Treatment Issues. In Services for Children of Alcoholics, NIAAA Research Monograph 4, 1979.

Whitfield, C.L.: Co-Alcoholism: Recognizing a Treatable Illness. Family and Community Health, Vol. 7, Summer, 1984.

Whitfield, C.L.: Co-Dependence: Our Most Common Addiction. Alcoholism Treatment Quarterly 6:1, 1989.

Whitfield, C.L.: A Gift to Myself: A Personal Workbook & Guide To Healing My Child Within. Health Communcations, Deerfield Beach, Florida, 1990.

Whitfield, C.L.: Alcoholism and Spirituality. Perrin & Tregett 1-800-321-7912, Rutherford, N.J., 1985.

Wilber, K.: No Boundary. Shambhala, Boston, Massachusetts, 1979.

Wilber, K.: Eye to Eye: The Quest for a New Paradigm. Anchor/ Doubleday, Garden City, New York, 1983.

Williams, S.K.: The Practice of Personal Transformation. Journey Press, Berkeley, California, 1985.

Winnicott, D.W.: Collected Papers. Basic Books, New York, 1958.

Woititz, J.G.: Struggle for Intimacy. Health Communications, Pompano Beach, Florida, 1985.

Woititz, J.G.: Adult Children of Alcoholics. Health Communications, Pompano Beach, Florida, 1983.

Order Form For A Gift To Myself

SHIPPING/HANDLING — All orders shipped UPS unless weight exceeds 200 lbs., special routing is requested or delivery territory is outside continental U.S. Orders outside United States shipped either Air Parcel Post or Surface Parcel Post. Shipping and handling charges apply to all orders shipped via UPS, Book Rate, Library Rate, Air or surface Parcel Post or Common Carrier and will be charged as follows, unless Common Carrier <u>collect</u> is requested.

TOTAL ORDER VALUE (After Discounts)	ADD
Less than $25.00	$2.00 minimum OR
$25.00-$50.00	$2.50 minimum OR
over $50.00 in the U.S.	6% of value
over $50.00 outside the U.S.	15% of value

Note: Do not include applicable sales taxes in the calculation of the value of your order for shipping/handling purposes.

DISCOUNT SCHEDULE: Items CAN be mixed to achieve quantity breaks. Items purchased at a discount that are returned will be credited against your account at the highest discount provided.

QUANTITY DISCOUNT	
20-99 copies	— 20%
100-299 copies	— 30%
300+ copies	— 40%

	PRICE	QUANTITY	TO
A Gift To Myself	$11.95	_____	____

Total amount of order = $ _____

Less any applicable discount - $ _____

Plus sales tax of 6% for FL residents + $ _____

GRAND TOTAL ENCLOSED = $ _____

Ship my prepaid order to:

Name: _____

Address: _____

_____

City: _____

State: _____ Zip: _____

Save Time: Call 800-851-9100
For Credit Card Orders

Charge this order to my ☐ Mastercard ☐ Visa

Signature _____

Card Number: _____

Expires: _____

Daytime Phone Number: ( ) _____ - _____